守株待兔

*Watching the Tree
to Catch a Hare*

Watching the Tree to Catch a Hare

守 株 待 兔

A Chinese daughter reflects on happiness,
spiritual beliefs and universal wisdom

ADELINE YEN MAH

HarperCollins*Publishers*

HarperCollins*Publishers*
77–85 Fulham Palace Road,
Hammersmith, London W6 8JB
www.**fire**and**water**.com

Published by HarperCollins*Publishers* 2000
1 3 5 7 9 8 6 4 2

A catalogue record for this book
is available from the British Library

ISBN 0-00-257099-8

Set in PostScript Linotype Photina and Electra by
Rowland Phototypesetting Ltd,
Bury St Edmunds, Suffolk

Printed and bound in Great Britain by
Clays Ltd, St Ives plc

CONTENTS

DEDICATED TO
MY GRANDFATHER
YEN QIAN LI
嚴乾利

(1878–1952)

I wish to thank my Ye Ye and honour him in
Watching the Tree.
His memory continues to give me strength.
I hope his teaching will be of help to some who are
also searching for spiritual tranquillity and solace.

To my husband and best friend, Bob,
without whom this book could not have been written.
To our mentor Mason Wang,
for his help in the Chinese classics.
To our daughter Ann Mah,
for her encouragement.
To Zhang Qing-Ying,
for her beautiful calligraphy.

1

Watching the Tree to Catch a Hare

守株待兔

SHOU ZHU DAI TU

My grandfather (Ye Ye) and I shared a rapport that neither of us ever verbalised during his lifetime. He was a businessman but was more interested in books than money. As a little girl in Shanghai, I spent hours playing by myself on the balcony attached to his room. Through the French windows I could see him practising calligraphy, writing letters or consulting the *I Ching*. Sometimes, he would let me 'help' him make fresh ink by grinding the ink-stick on an antique stone slab left to him by his father. I did not inherit Ye Ye's artistic talent and was in awe of his *shu fa* 書法 (calligraphy).

As the youngest stepdaughter in a Chinese family of seven children, I knew I was unwanted and considered by my family to be the lowest of the low. At home, my misery filled my whole world. It was real and deep and I could see no way out, possessing neither the wisdom nor the cynicism to blunt the cruelty and the constant rejection.

When I was ten, my stepmother Niang separated me from

my aunt, whom I dearly loved, and placed me in a succession of Catholic boarding schools. I was unaware that all my mail (both incoming and outgoing) was being sent to my parents for censoring. I only knew that I never heard from my aunt or anyone else for the next four years.

During that time I had nobody but my grandfather. Although I was only allowed 'home' on three separate occasions, I treasured those brief visits. I did not know then how vital they were to my emotional and spiritual development.

The Swedish psychologist Eric Ericson wrote of a sense of basic trust, which is instilled in a child by 'somebody who cares', without which the child cannot live and dies mentally. This 'basic trust' was what my Ye Ye gave to me at that crucial juncture. During the many years when I was isolated in the boarding school in Hong Kong, I was sustained only by my inner conviction that my Ye Ye loved me. At times, things were very bad. My stepmother had a way of making me feel like nothing; a piece of garbage to be thrown away. But, through it all, the thought of my Ye Ye would return and revive my spirits at odd moments. Deep inside, I knew I mattered to him and that he believed in me.

Many decades passed before I came to recognise the depth of his influence. His thoughts were pivotal in shaping me into the person I became. This book is a letter of gratitude to a grandfather who once gave me the most precious of all gifts: my sense of hope.

At the dawn of our new millennium there is a hunger in people throughout the world to comprehend who we are and how we fit together. As a result, interest in eastern philosophy is growing in the west. One quarter of the world's population lives in China, eats with chopsticks and speaks Chinese. As products of the oldest living civilisation whose culture and language have survived virtually intact, Chinese philosophy, beliefs and wisdom have much to offer. *Watching the Tree* is concerned with Chinese thought and the reason why we Chinese think the way we do. In it, I have used many incidents from my life to illustrate certain Chinese concepts and related what I have learnt from them.

In my first book, *Falling Leaves*, I reported my Aunt Baba's words when we were reunited after a separation of thirty years.

'The way I see it [she said], the nineteenth century was a British century. The twentieth century is an American century. I predict that the twenty-first century will be a Chinese century. The pendulum of history will swing from the *yin* ashes brought by the Cultural Revolution to the *yang* phoenix arising from its wreckage.'

Having lived and worked as a physician in California for thirty years, I consider myself Chinese-American and am very fond of my adopted country. My aunt, however, was born in 1905 and still saw the world through lenses moulded by China's humiliations during the two preceding centuries. From the dawn of history, we Chinese had regarded China as the centre of the world, and considered every other nation to be barbaric. In 1842 China lost the Opium War and Hong Kong was ceded to Britain. Subsequently China endured 150 years of foreign exploitation and coastal cities such as Shanghai and Tianjin came under foreign control. My grandparents, parents and aunt were all born in the French Concession of Shanghai, where they were ruled by Frenchmen under French law and lived as second-class citizens in their own native city. Perhaps as a consequence, my grandfather, aunt and father used to view all westerners with a mixture of awe and resentment.

After Sun Yat-sen toppled the imperial Qing dynasty in 1911, China became a republic. The country soon broke up into fiefdoms ruled by warlords, who fought the Japanese as well as each other for control. Chiang Kai-shek, a military general and protégé of Sun Yat-sen, united the country after Sun's death but was forced to escape to Taiwan when he lost the civil war to the Communists under Mao Zedong in 1949. Mao drove out the foreigners along with the Nationalists, proclaimed the founding of the People's Republic and, on 1 October 1949, declared from the Gate of Heavenly Peace in Beijing that 'the Chinese people have finally stood up for themselves', meaning that China was no longer subject to foreign rule.

From 1949 until his death in 1976 Mao was essentially China's one-man dictator. My aunt compared him to Qin Shi Huang Di, the 'terracotta army' emperor who united China in 221 BC and whose power and cruelty were legendary. Under Mao's reign, love of the motherland was the highest virtue on earth. In its name rested sanctity, salvation and a purpose of life. Nationalism replaced Confucianism, Taoism and Buddhism as the Chinese people worshipped at the altar of Mao. China remained isolated, backward and undeveloped for the twenty-seven years under Mao's rule. The Cultural Revolution (1966–72) was unleashed by Mao to topple his enemies and to free the country of the 'four olds' – habits, customs, ideals and creeds. Instead, it wiped out all traditional codes of

4

beliefs and produced a bewildered generation of Red Guards. Even today, there are those within China who preach xenophobia, isolationism, protectionism and resistance to modern market policy. A case of Maoism versus the Disney-fication of China.

Following the break-up of the Soviet Union, the USA is the only superpower left on the world arena today. The dominance of America stems primarily from a philosophy of private enterprise that underpins its economic, educational and political systems. Although China is the world's most populous country, with 1.3 billion people, it is only one of many ascending nations jockeying for position. Asian countries such as Japan, Korea, Malaysia, India and Pakistan have all undergone industrialisation and modernisation within the last fifty years. Our whole world is already a fusion of east and west; around the globe we are becoming ever more closely linked by ties of environment, security, trade and information. It is now vital for all our futures that we gain an understanding of each other's history, language and culture.

When I was thirteen years old, my stepmother informed me that I was to leave my school in Hong Kong the following year and get a job because my father could no longer afford my school fees. Desperate to get further education, I confided to my grandfather Ye Ye that I was considering running away secretly to join my Aunt Baba back in Shanghai. Would he consider lending me the fare?

'What will you do in Shanghai?' he asked.

'Go back to my old school. I can't wait to see all my old classmates again. When my parents took me away from my Shanghai school three years ago, I had just been elected class

5

president. Do you think they will still let me be class president when I go back?'

Grandfather looked at me with a peculiar expression. 'So you think everything in Shanghai will be exactly the same as when you left? How childish you are! Have you forgotten again what it says over and over in the *I Ching*? The only thing that does not change is that everything changes.

'Let me tell you a story that I hope you'll never forget. Once there was a boy who was told by his master to catch a hare. He went into the woods and looked around. Lo and behold, at that very moment, he saw a hare running along at full speed. As he watched in astonishment, the hare ran smack into a tree and knocked itself unconscious. All he had to do was to pick it up. For the rest of his life the boy waited behind the same tree in the hope that more hares would do the same thing.

'That boy is like you, expecting the same conditions to be waiting when you return to your school in Shanghai. Watching the tree to catch a hare (守株待兔 *sho zhu dai tu*)!'

That was one of the last conversations I had with my grandfather. He died a few months later.

Did my grandfather make up this story? No. Who wrote it? A philosopher named Han Fei Tzu 韓非子. When did he live? Over 2000 years ago. He died in 233 BC.

After the publication of *Falling Leaves* many readers wrote to ask me: 'Given the fact that China was so much more advanced than other civilisations up to the time of Marco Polo (Yuan dynasty – 1260–1368), why did it fall behind the west from then on?'

There are many theories put forward to explain China's

decline. Mine is very simple and is based on one word: education. In the chapter on Confucius I discuss how, for over 2000 years, the sole purpose of education in China was to study the works of Confucius so as to pass the imperial civil examinations and become a magistrate. The study of astronomy (*tian wen* 天文) by the general public was restricted because only the emperor (and his appointees at the Bureau of Astronomy) had the right to study the stars. The importance of mathematics in the study of science was never recognised in Imperial China. Mathematics was considered a waste of time since it did not help one to pass the examinations. Potential Chinese Keplers, Galileos and Newtons were busy memorising Confucian texts. Mathematical language based on the Hindu-Arabic numerical system was not generally adopted until the twentieth century. During my father's youth in the twenties and thirties calculations were still being carried out on the abacus because Chinese numbers (like Roman numerals) lack two essential elements: *zero* and *position*, both of which are implied on the abacus but become invisible when the numbers are transcribed on to paper in Chinese characters. Without an adequate numerical alphabet, mathematical thought could not advance and science could not develop.

During the nineteenth century, the Industrial Revolution freed man from the drudgery of manual labor, but the information revolution taking place now will cause far more radical revisions, because it is unleashing the power and expanding the dimension of man's minds.

In terms of material wealth and scientific progress, achievements in the west have been undisputedly awesome in the last two hundred years. But, has western prosperity brought westerners inner contentment and genuine satisfaction? When desire for money takes precedence over human relationships, can one be truly happy?

Throughout the world people are yearning for spiritual inspiration as well as for a purpose to their lives. Nowhere is this search more urgent than in China where, since the death of Mao, people have become increasingly desperate to find religious meaning and substance. The success of cults such as Falun Gong reflects this hunger. Many are seeking alternatives to materialism, science, Communism and the institutional religions.

When I was eleven years old my parents placed me in a Catholic convent in Hong Kong as a boarder. Soon I came under the influence of Catholic nuns and was quoting the Bible. During one of my rare visits home I discussed my newfound faith with my grandfather (Ye Ye) and he compared our respective beliefs.

'As a Chinese from the old school, I have always had difficulty sticking to any one religion,' Ye Ye said. 'Even though I believe in reincarnation because I am a Buddhist, I honour my ancestors and read the *I Ching* and the *Tao Te Ching* 道德經. All my educated friends behave similarly.

'Unlike Muhammadans or Christians, we Chinese have trouble with the western view that there is only one true God. Why can't Muhammad be accepted as a prophet as well as Moses? Why does one belief have to exclude another? Why can't all the religions merge together and become one?

'As a boy, your father got into big trouble with an American firm once because he wrote on his job application form next to "Religion?": "Catholic, but willing to become Methodist as well, if necessary." The manager summoned him into his office and called him a "rice Christian", ready to turn his back on Catholicism for a job with a Protestant firm.

'"Why must there be only one true sect?" your father protested. "Why can't I be a Catholic as well as a Methodist? Why can't I be both?"

'But the American manager was angry and your father didn't get the job. So he moved to Tianjin and worked for me instead.'

In the following chapters I shall outline the differences between east and west on a number of fundamental topics. Because some Chinese words are non-existent in English, just as various English words are absent in Chinese, the only way in which to grasp certain concepts that are unique to China is by leaping across national barriers and allowing for the possibility that truth may be reached in a language other than one's own.

One Chinese book which will open realms of thought beyond the usual western parameters of perception is the *I Ching*. Other ideas that play dominant roles in Chinese thinking are Confucianism, Taoism and Zen Buddhism. I illustrate traditional concepts such as *qi, feng shui* and *yin/yang* with incidents from my personal life. In each case I hope to bridge the cultural divide between east and west, so that westerners will be able to understand the Chinese way of thinking, discover its roots and see how they resemble or differ from their own. Having spent my first fourteen years in China, and the rest of my life in England and America, I can understand the mind set of both world views.

When my father sent me to study in England in the 1950s, there were few Chinese students in Europe or America. Nowadays, more and more are migrating to the west in search of education, freedom, prosperity and happiness. Deregulation of telecommunications, growth of international trade, ease of air travel and the Internet will ensure increasing contact between east and west. Many childless would-be parents from America are adopting unwanted Chinese baby girls. Intermarriage is also on the rise. My own son married a Brazilian woman whose parents came from Austria and they have an adorable baby boy. The destiny of such infants will write a new chapter in the future relationship between China and the west.

What will that destiny be? The proverb *shou zhu dai tu* 守株待兔 teaches us that change is the only constant. To that, I will add also the universal human yearning for truth and wisdom. For me, this yearning has no borders; it is as urgent a need in America as in China. Given that, and my spiritual and emotional citizenship in both countries, I have written *Watching the Tree* to present many traditional Chinese beliefs to my fellow constituents: the students of the world.

Religion and spirituality are ambiguous words with widely differing interpretations. *Watching the Tree* attempts to deal with these terms on a scientific and rational basis, without dogma or superstition. The great German philosopher Martin Heidegger once wrote, 'Whatever and however we may try to think, we think within the sphere of tradition.' But what if I were to introduce to western readers a new and entirely different tradition? Could their thoughts become transformed and undergo fresh and radical change?

Philosophy starts with wonder and knowledge is power. Aristotle said, 'All men by nature desire to know.' Indeed, Chinese and Westerners alike are all searching for rational and intelligent answers. Somewhere it is written that every Chinese wears a Confucian thinking-cap, Taoist robe and Buddhist sandals. Like my two previous books, *Watching the Tree* is autobiographical and gives you a glimpse into a Chinese mind. You can see the basis of my personal philosophy and the reason why I think the way I do. I hope it will provide you with an introduction to eastern thought, one that you can use as a stepping stone on your individual path towards the development of your own beliefs.

Enjoy! I wish you happiness.

2

Light at the End of the Tunnel

否極泰來

PI JI TAI LAI

Like many Chinese scholars, my grandfather (Ye Ye) was an ardent follower of the *I Ching*. He viewed it as his Bible: a book of wisdom as well as a book of divination. A few months after his death from diabetes, I came across his copy of the *I Ching* and a small bundle of sticks wrapped together in a piece of red silk. At first I thought the sticks were chopsticks but they were too thin even though they were all of equal length. Later I discovered that they were stalks from the yarrow plant.

We were living in Hong Kong and I had been allowed to come home from boarding school to prepare for my forth-coming education in England. It was the first time I had been home since Ye Ye's funeral. I was sleeping in his old room and it was still full of his belongings and the odour of his cigars. Although I was euphoric at the imminent prospect of going away to a new school in a foreign land far from my stepmother, I missed my grandfather. The sight of his much-thumbed copy of the *I Ching*, yellow with age, brought a sudden pang that caused the tears to course down my cheeks. On opening its cover, I saw his name, Yen Qian Li 嚴乾利, and the year Guang Xu 21 (1896) written with brush and ink. He was then eighteen years old and his calligraphy seemed to shimmer with all the hope and joy of youth. Knowing that my stepmother planned to discard his books and redecorate his room, I packed the tattered volume into my trunk and took it to Oxford with me.

Ten years passed. I graduated from medical school in London and was mired in a tormented relationship with my tutor, Professor Decker. Karl was a bachelor, sixteen years older than I, and already established in his scientific career. It was an impossible affair: Karl would vacillate from day to day between commitment and escape. Although he had warned me about his emotional instability, I was convinced I could weather his depressions and make him happy. He was terrified of marriage but tempted by my youthful optimism. His rejections were invariably followed by lengthy poetic letters tinged with love and regret – letters that bound me to him even as he verbally protested that we had to part.

This situation continued for seven years. I took a job in Edinburgh to distance myself physically from him. His letters followed and I began to live for them. One Sunday morning, as I lay in bed listening to the church bells ringing and feeling forlorn, I glanced up at my bookshelf and saw my Ye Ye's copy of the *I Ching* leaning against the cardboard box in which I stored Karl's letters. In the ten years since I had left Hong Kong I had never once opened the ragged tome. Under Karl's influence, I now considered myself a westernised intellectual and had nothing but contempt for ancient Chinese books of divination.

I took the book down and saw with it the bundle of sticks

neatly bound with a cord. They were stored in a special pouch sewn ingeniously on to the book's cloth binding. On the back cover was a list of instructions on how to use the *I Ching*. The reader was informed that within the bundle there were fifty yarrow stalks as well as two sticks of incense. Yarrow, or milfoil, was a common plant in China and its stalks had been used since ancient times for purposes of divination. The incense was to be replaced after each reading.

Randomly, I flipped through the pages: the book consisted of sixty-four hexagrams (卦 *gua*: see page 19), the margins of which were annotated in many places by my grandfather's familiar handwriting. Next to no. 29 (坎 *kan*), he had written '*pi ji tai lai*' (light at the end of the tunnel).

Curious and excited, I began to read:

> The hexagram *kan* ䷜ consists of two identical trigrams also named *kan* ☵, one on top and one at the bottom. A *yang* line (continuous line) __ lies between two *yin* lines (interrupted lines) ⚏. *Kan* represents the heart locked within the body. Because *kan* is repeated twice in this hexagram, it means 'repetition of danger'.
>
> The word *kan* 坎 denotes 'plunging in'. A *yang* line __ has plunged in and is enclosed by two *yin* lines ☵ like water in a ravine. This hexagram represents an objective situation that is very dangerous. It is a situation in which one is trapped as water is trapped in a ravine. Like water, a person can escape only if he behaves resolutely and with appropriate caution.

Thoroughly intrigued, I turned to the beginning. 'This ancient book of wisdom,' I read, 'may be of help at moments of indecision. Treat it with reverence. Follow the directions meticulously. Phrase your question carefully. Receive the answer respectfully. Ponder its significance and act according to its guidance.'

For some reason, at that moment, the words seemed momentous: like a message sent by my grandfather from beyond his grave, delivered at that instant for a particular purpose. After studying the instructions, I followed them scrupulously. I bathed and dressed as if I was going to church, then made my bed, cleaned the room, locked my door and unplugged my telephone. Feeling somewhat foolish, I placed my bedspread on the floor, arranged the *I Ching*, a piece of paper and pen, a vase of flowers (brought by Karl on his recent visit) and the fifty yarrow stalks neatly next to each other.

I lit the incense and sat cross-legged on a cushion facing the bedspread. Then I closed my eyes and thought of the last seven years with Karl, remembering the sweetness as well as the pain. After much deliberation, I wrote my question. 'Will you please give me guidance as to how I should behave in my relationship with Karl?'

Next I started dividing the yarrow stalks exactly as instructed. Though simple, it was a protracted process that took almost an hour. During that time many thoughts went through my mind. Did my Ye Ye ever have such a relationship? Was he at times also unhappy? Why did he write the words '*pi ji tai lai*' next to hexagram no. 29? Will I be able to survive without Karl? Or will I be happier alone?

I found myself talking to my dead grandfather and imagining his answers. Am I going crazy? I thought. What would Karl say if he saw me now – his pupil (the would-be scientist) burning incense and having a dialogue with an ancient book purported to possess spiritual authority! Am I performing an act of ancestor-worship?

Finally, I completed the procedure: having manipulated the stalks I came up with six lines of numbers. After consulting the chart at the back of the book, I found *gua* no. 44 (☴ *kou*). 'The hexagram *kou*,' I read, 'denotes a predicament in which darkness creeps back furtively after being eliminated. Of its own volition, the female arrives to meet the male. It is highly unlucky and dangerous and one must act promptly to prevent possible disaster.'

I wrote the answer next to my question to the *I Ching*. I felt the hair rising at the back of my neck as I read and re-read the phrases interpreting the hexagram *kou*. In all sincerity, I had asked my question and the answer was unequivocal. I must resolve to destroy Karl's love letters and leave England as soon as possible. I must act promptly to prevent disaster and never go back. There was no doubt in my mind that the *I Ching*'s advice was sound.

That Sunday morning in Edinburgh was the only occasion I ever consulted the *I Ching*. After lunch I spent the day in bed reading the rest of the book. As I read, I remember being astonished by the many astute, profound and noble ideas conceived thousands of years ago. For a few hours that day, the book came alive and spoke to me personally. I could almost hear my grandfather exhorting me to continue searching for guidance from his favourite book.

Afterwards, all through the agony of breaking free, I would re-read my hexagram every time I wavered. Not only did it point to a course of action I needed to follow, it sustained me throughout the ordeal. At our final parting Karl asked for a token by which to remember our years together. I rewrapped

17

my grandfather's *I Ching* in its original silk and mailed it to him. For me, Ye Ye's book had become a symbol of deliverance. By giving it to Karl I was declaring my independence ... but I never did tell him what happened that morning in Edinburgh between the *I Ching* and me.

In China the *I Ching* has long been considered to be the oldest book in the world and a great classic, as well as the foundation of Chinese scholarship. Indeed, it seems to transcend time and national boundaries, providing perennial significance and solace. The ideas it contains have continued to play a dominant role in Chinese thinking from ancient times to the present. It is thought to have been written over 4000 years ago, but its exact age is unknown. The great seventeenth-century German mathematician Gottfried von Leibniz called it 'the oldest monument of scholarship'. To Carl Jung, it was 'the experimental foundation of classical Chinese philosophy'.

Legend attributes the authorship to Fu Xi* 伏羲 (2953– 2838 BC), an ancient and mythical king of China who supposedly led his people into the age of agriculture. In ancient times the book was used for the purposes of divination: words from the *I Ching* were inscribed on bones known as 'oracle bones', some of which were discovered at the turn of the twentieth century.

Much later, around 1150 BC, King Wen 文王, the founder of the Chou dynasty, rearranged the hexagrams (more on this later: see page 20). He also wrote the judgements (or commentaries) known as *Gua T'uan* 卦彖 on the hexagrams.

---

* A legendary figure, who may never have existed.

One of King Wen's sons, the Duke of Chou 周公, composed the *Hsiao T'uan* 爻象 to expand these judgements.

The title, *I Ching*, is known in English as *The Book of Changes*. The word *I* 易, pronounced *yi*, means 'changes'. This may have arisen from the ancient Chinese character for the lizard or chameleon, 𧈢, which is known for changing its colour. A lizard can also drop its tail and grow another. The second word, *Ching* 經 (pronounced *jing*), means 'classic' or 'book'.

Divination was practised in ancient China for thousands of years. Initially, it was done by incising a tortoise shell with a red-hot stylus until the shell cracked. The diviner then foretold the future by reading the cracked lines. Later, the ancient rulers consulted the *I Ching* by clustering and dividing yarrow stalks.

The use of the *I Ching* for such occult purposes aroused suspicion and scorn in many scholars, including Confucius (born 551 BC), who had nothing but contempt for the practice. Having studied the book carefully for many years, Confucius said as he neared the end of his life, 'If my life were to be prolonged, I would use fifty years to study the *I Ching*; so that I might escape falling into grave errors.' He and his disciples subsequently wrote ten appendices (十翼 *shi yi*) to interpret and clarify the main text of the *I Ching*. These appendices were strongly influenced by Taoism and expressed sentiments similar to those contained in Lao Zi's *Book of Tao* (see page 35).

The text of the *I Ching* consists of sixty-four short essays (opinions or 'judgements') on important moral, social, psychological and philosophical themes. Each essay is represented by a different symbol known as a *gua*. *Gua* is one of those Chinese words which has no exact English equivalent. A rough translation would be 'emblem of divine guidance and wisdom'. The closest example of a *gua* in the west would be the sign of the cross. In 1854 a British sinologist named James Legge translated the word *gua* (as used in the *I Ching*) into English as 'trigram' or 'hexagram'. A trigram ☰ consists of a stack of three short straight lines, whereas a hexagram ䷏ is made of two trigrams or a stack of six lines. These lines may be divided (broken), undivided (joined) or a mixture of divided and undivided. Every trigram and hexagram has its own name.

Altogether there are eight possible trigrams and sixty-four hexagrams which, with the ten appendices, supposedly represent every possible human situation that can occur in life.

The *I Ching* contains certain basic and important Chinese concepts. Among them is *yin/yang*, or the 'Dualist' theory. According to this theory, everything in the universe is divided according to the *yin* or the *yang*. However, *yin* and *yang* are neither competitive nor exclusionist. On the contrary, the two are complementary, interdependent and eventually transform into one another. They are each other's universal counterparts. This notion may have been derived originally from the experience of 'day and night' as well as 'winter and summer'.

Yin 陰 means 'shady side of a hill', and is associated with such words as female, moon, darkness, night, negative *qi*, or spirit of earth (see page 138), water, absorbent; it is represented by a divided (broken) line in a trigram or hexagram.

Yang 陽 means 'bright side of a hill', and is identified with such words as male, sun, light, day, positive *qi*, or spirit of Heaven (see page 141), fire, creative power; it is indicated by an undivided (joined) line in a trigram or hexagram.

Yin/yang is also represented by two fish in a circle. The drawing is called Tai-ji Tu 太極圖 or Diagram of the Great Ultimate. One fish is black with a white dot in it. The other

is white with a black dot in it. *Yin* cannot exist without *yang* and vice versa. Without night there can be no day. Without black there can be no white. Inside every *yin* there is a little bit of *yang*. Inside every *yang* there is a certain degree of *yin*. (This diagram has been adopted as the national flag of South Korea.)

According to Cheng Yi 程頤 (1033–1107) of the Song dynasty,

> *Yin* and *yang* are everywhere. In front and behind. To our left and to our right. Above us and below us. Darkness is the same as diminished light. Light is the same as diminished darkness. They are complementary. Universal counterparts. *Yin* does not exist without *yang* and *yang* does not exist without *yin*. Two in one and one in two.

Another important concept in the *I Ching* is that of *wu xing* 五行, the five elements, five forces or five phases. These are wood, fire, earth, metal and water. They correlate with the five directions (north, south, east, west and centre); the five seasons (spring, summer, earth, autumn and winter); and the five colours, senses, tones, flavours, classics, etc.

On a Chinese map, south is depicted at the top of a circular chart and is associated with fire and summer. East is on the left and corresponds to wood (and growth) and spring. West is to the right and is associated with metal and autumn. North is at the bottom and represents water and winter. At the centre of the circle is the earth. Each direction or season is not unchanging but one phase follows the other continuously.

These five forces or phases are supposed to guide and control all natural phenomena. Sequentially, wood produces fire; fire produces earth (ashes); ashes produce metal (ore is extracted from the earth); metal produces water (dew is deposited on a metal mirror); water produces wood (makes possible the growth of wood). Conversely, water extinguishes fire; fire melts metal; metal cuts wood; wood penetrates earth by the use of the wooden plough; earth soaks up the course of water. The cycle is completed.

The number 5 is very popular in Chinese culture. A teaset frequently consists of a teapot and five cups. Chinese politicians often promise to accomplish five goals during their term in office. When President Nixon visited China in 1972, the Chinese Premier Zhou Enlai outlined five non-negotiable points before meaningful dialogue could begin.

Yin and *yang* and the five forces form the basis of Chinese thought. They underpin many traditional Chinese patterns of life such as *feng shui* ('wind and water' or geomancy), which is practised when purchasing a home, an office or a burial site; exercises such as *qi gong* and *tai chi*; the choice of foods; the practice of Chinese medicine; and religious beliefs such as Taoism and Buddhism. I shall expand on all these themes later in the book.

Before the twentieth century man perceived all matter as being composed of material particles whose movements were governed by partial differential equations and Newton's laws of thermodynamics. Western man was preoccupied with causally sequenced events. He was out to conquer nature and fight the forces of evil. The world was thought to be as either *for* him or *against* him. Things were black or white. Death was the enemy of life.

These days, physical reality is represented by continuous fields governed by partial differential equations. At the sub-atomic realm, Newtonian physics has been replaced by quantum mechanics and the 'super-string' theory. Matter and energy are interchangeable. Time and space are no longer separate realities but complementary to each other. The three dimensions of space have incorporated a fourth dimension: space/time.

At the beginning of the twenty-first century our thinking seems to be veering towards the teachings of the *I Ching*. In contrast to the thinking of the twentieth century, we now agree with the ancient Chinese philosophers that our world is neither static nor absolute. Everything is relative, as in the duality of *yin* and *yang*. Change is the only given, nothing remains the same, and all standards are relative. We are born, we mature, grow old and die. Then the cycle begins again. Life and death are but temporary manifestations of the same central reality. Midnight at home just means midday somewhere else. Only the fact of change itself is unchanging. Eventually, everything will return to the beginning of all things – to the *tao* (way) or Divine Intelligence of the Universe – because that is how the cycle began initially.

Perhaps it is this belief that no state is permanent but that the pace of change cannot be forced that gives us Chinese our forbearance. I remember being shocked and saddened by my aunt's poverty and dismal surroundings when I visited her in Shanghai in 1979. She had been driven out of her home by

Red Guards during the Cultural Revolution in 1966 and was forced to live in one small room in a neighbour's house. When I invited her out to lunch, she asked permission to take a bath in our hotel room. She was in the bathroom for so long that I went in to check on her. I found her luxuriating in the tub staring at the ceiling. 'Are you all right?' I asked. 'You have no idea,' she answered, 'how delicious it feels to lie in warm water like this unless you have been deprived of a proper bath for thirteen years. It feels so good that it was almost worth the deprivation to have this hour of bliss.' Then she added, 'Things are bound to change for the better now. This too will pass. I must not despair when life gets too hard nor be too complacent when I'm too comfortable.'

The German mathematician and philosopher Gottfried Wilhelm Leibniz (1646–1716), the inventor of calculus, was introduced to the *I Ching* through his friendship with the Jesuit priest Father Joachim Bouvet, who served as a missionary in China. Bouvet showed Leibniz the diagram drawn by Shao Yung 邵雍 (a Song dynasty scholar), an arrangement of the sixty-four hexagrams. When told that the hexagrams were analogous to seeds containing all the potential answers to everything in the universe, Leibniz said of Fu Xi, author of the *I Ching*, 'He is the founder of scholarship in China and the Far East. His *I Ching* table, handed down to the world, is the oldest monument of scholarship.'

Looking at the hexagrams of the *I Ching*, Leibniz recognised his own system of binary mathematics in the symbols by representing *yin* 陰 (the broken line) as zero and *yang* 陽 (the unbroken line) as one. Thus a hexagram ䷀ with one divided (*yin*) line and five undivided (*yang*) lines would have the sequence of numbers 011111; whereas a hexagram ☳ with one undivided (*yang*) line and five divided (*yin*) lines would produce 100000. Some scholars suggest that Leibniz was inspired by Shao Yung's diagram to invent binary mathematics in the first place.

In our time, both the number system in computer science and Larry Fullerton's recently patented digital pulse technology use Leibniz's binary mathematics to carry out their functions. Like the computer, the *I Ching* was also designed by 'wise men' as a mechanism to facilitate man's thinking in processing information. Aptly, *I Ching* has been nicknamed the 'poor man's computer', the 'archetypal computer' and the 'most archaic computer'.

Carl Jung began studying the *I Ching* during the late nineteenth century and continued to consult it frequently until his death in 1961. Jung viewed the conscious and the unconscious as having a correlating function in man's behaviour, where the unconscious normally plays a complementary role to the conscious. Occasionally, however, this becomes impossible and then the unconscious is forced to be the adversary of the conscious, thereby causing inner conflict.

Undoubtedly, there are moments in our lives when we find ourselves stuck at a psychological impasse. Inside, we are in turmoil yet we are unwilling to admit the problem to ourselves, let alone discuss it with anyone else.

At such times, the conscious and unconscious may become successfully reunited through psychotherapy. It is important, however, that the patient in search of peace of mind be healed as a whole person, not treated merely for a particular symptom. Carl Jung agreed with the *I Ching* that there is a little *yin* (female) energy in every male and a little *yang* (male) energy in every female. He advised a holistic approach in treating patients, calling it 'the process of individuation through a creative integration of opposites'. The key to success, according to Jung, was to make the patient aware of his unconscious as he goes about his conscious everyday life.

Jungian psychotherapy aims to reveal to the patient certain vague and unformed primordial images which may have manifested themselves in his dreams and fantasies. It is none other than a symbolic quest for his unconscious. The sixty-four hexagrams in the *I Ching* have been considered by some to be the union of psychic opposites. Each hexagram is composed of two trigrams. This combination may be seen as representing the union of the unconscious (inner trigram) and the conscious (outer trigram).

Consulting the I Ching

From time to time we all get stuck in difficult psychological situations. The Chinese recognised many centuries ago that the human mind is often over-burdened and confused. At those moments, the *I Ching* may offer a way out by providing a method of self-examination. Its hexagrams are symbols conveying messages which form the basis for meaning and substance in our human existence. These hexagrams can be randomly selected at any given moment. Each represents a specific instant in a continuous cycle of change. They explain and articulate certain inner truths about subjects which, on some occasions, many of us hate to admit or even think about: separation, divorce, death – and the attendant wills and legacies. My grandfather once told me that many elderly men of his father's generation used to consult the *I Ching* before they wrote their wills.

In order to consult the *I Ching* properly and with a clear mind while avoiding the possibility of influence by the occult or the divine, one should follow a few simple rules:

Find a quiet, tidy room. Bathe and dress in comfortable clothes. Be alone. Lock the door. Take the phone off the hook.

Formulate your question to the *I Ching* carefully. Describe your problem or symptom. Spend time thinking about it. Write it down as succinctly and accurately as possible.

The number of the hexagram which will 'answer' your question can be found by either tossing a coin or dividing yarrow sticks. I recommend the latter – not because I believe in 'black magic' but because the ritual of dividing the sticks solemnises the occasion. It also takes longer. Coin-tossing takes about two minutes whereas dividing sticks may take from twenty to sixty minutes. During this time your mind should be concentrating on the question at hand. Some people burn incense to put themselves in the mood. The occasion should not be treated frivolously but with reverence and sincerity. It provides a period of self-examination and meditation, comparable to attending mass or going to confession.

If you can, use the Wilhelm/Baynes translation of the *I Ching* (published by Princeton University Press in 1990). Unfortunately, Chinese is a very imprecise language, without gender, tense or numbers (see page 167). Classic Chinese as written in ancient times is particularly difficult to understand. What you get out of the *I Ching* depends very much on your personal interpretation of the translator's explanations and commentaries on the hexagrams you have located in answer to your questions. The whole process is something like looking at Rorschach's ink-blots. What you eventually see will be a projection of your own latent thoughts.

Contemplate and reflect on the hexagram you've arrived at and its interpretation. Consulting the *I Ching* is really an occasion for soul-searching and self-analysis. For believers, this is the time for your private conversation with God. For sceptics, this is an opportunity to have the candid dialogue with yourself which you have been avoiding. Use it to clarify your life and unearth your hidden motives. I recommend that you write down the *I Ching*'s conclusions and prescriptions on the same sheet of paper as your question. Even if no one ever reads it but you, you will find the whole writing process enormously satisfying and cathartic. For those who have been hurt and are in need of spiritual solace, contemplation and reflection are excellent alternatives to anti-depressants, sleeping pills, electric shock treatments or psychiatric counselling. (The process is certainly less costly.) In fact, this may be the world's oldest method of self-administered bio-feedback, under the guidance of ancient Chinese wisdom.

The *I Ching* is not taught at school today and many Chinese have never heard of it. After that Sunday morning in Edinburgh, I myself never used it again, but doing research for this chapter brought back many memories. Did it help me? Definitely. Do I believe that my grandfather came back from the grave to guide me that day? No. However, going through the process of dividing the sticks and searching for the hexagram did make me examine truths I had not wished to acknowledge and provided me with a course of action I needed to follow.

3

Hidden and Nameless Tao

道隱無名

DAO YING WU MING

After I graduated from the London Hospital Medical School, I was fortunate enough to be chosen by the renowned neurologist Sir Russell Brain as his house-physician. One of the fringe benefits of working under Sir Russell was that it gave me the opportunity to treat his roster of famous private patients, many of whom suffered from unusual diseases that were difficult to diagnose. Among them was the great English poet Philip Larkin.

He was then close to forty, a balding man who worried about everything, with anxious intelligent eyes behind thick glasses. He had a private room and many vague symptoms: insomnia, deafness, lack of concentration, fainting spells. I was ordered to perform a plethora of painful diagnostic procedures on him which he endured without complaint. After each ordeal he would quiz me about the significance and rationale of the tests. On many occasions he would order the nurse in charge to page me 'immediately'. When I rushed back in response to his summons, I would find him listening to the radio or reading in bed, having forgotten he had sent for me.

We did, however, have some wonderful conversations: about literature, philosophy, poetry and the art of writing. I was in awe of his talent and flattered that he should want to chat with someone like me, a lowly intern with literary aspirations assigned to look after his health. Once he complained of boredom and asked whether I would consider having dinner with him outside the hospital on my day off. I declined and told him it was against hospital rules for house-physicians to socialise with their patients. 'The real reason is that there is someone special in your life, isn't there?' he asked. But I found his question difficult and left without answering.

We discussed music and I told him that my favourite composer was J. S. Bach. He mentioned a Dutch artist named Escher, whose drawings consisted of recurrent cyclical themes that reminded him of Bach's fugues and preludes. Then he asked me, 'What's the best book you've ever read?'

'Shakespeare's *King Lear*,' I answered without hesitation. 'What's yours?'

He started to laugh. 'It's almost too ironical. Here you are – a Chinese girl saying that the best book in the world, ever, is Shakespeare's *King Lear*. And here I am, an Englishman, telling you that it's the *Tao Te Ching** by Lao Zi 老子. Every word in that book matters. Nothing is superfluous. It's a work of absolute genius! Are you familiar with it? No?! I almost feel like learning Chinese just to be able to read it to you in the original. You must get hold of a copy! Most British libraries carry the Arthur Waley translation. Lao Zi delighted in writing in circles and

---

* Pronounced *Dao De Jing*.

paradoxes. You should read it while listening to Bach and looking at Escher's art. The works of all three have a common, revolving theme that somehow blends them with each other!'

Philip Larkin was discharged from hospital without a definite diagnosis. We said goodbye, and he gave me a copy of his poems, *The Less Deceived*, inscribing it to 'Dr Yen' and signing it 'With kindest regards from Philip Larkin'. A few months later, having completed my term as house-doctor, I moved to Edinburgh (as mentioned earlier) and went to work there. I took the book with me when I moved into the attic of Dennis and Helen Katz, colleagues and close friends of Karl's. However, Karl continued to write and his sporadic visits were deeply disturbing. At times, I thought I, too, would go mad. At the end of two years I finally made a clean break from Karl and went 'home' to my family in Hong Kong, leaving Larkin's book with the Katzes. On the publication of *Falling Leaves* three decades later I was doing a reading at the Edinburgh Festival when Dennis and Helen entered. In their hands they held a gift. They were returning Larkin's book.

I like to work in public libraries. While writing this chapter, I happened to be in the library on Brompton Road in London's Earls Court. Looking up from my manuscript one morning while searching for a word, I saw Anthony Thwaite's *Selected Letters of Philip Larkin, 1940–1985* standing on a shelf immediately above my desk. On a whim, I took the volume down and flipped through its pages, wondering if my former patient had described any of his experiences at the London Hospital. To my amazement and delight, I found my name mentioned in two of his letters to Maeve Brennan.

31

April 10, 1961 ... Everyone is very nice (my doctor, or rather, the house-doctor, is Chinese, a Miss Yen) ...

Well, now it is 9.45 and almost time for me to settle down for the night. Miss Yen came in and said the ear report was negative, so there's no cause to worry about *that*. Still, there are plenty of other things, aren't there. Miss Yen intimated that she couldn't hear what Sir Russell said either!* She keeps asking how one writes poetry, how one manages the beats and rhymes. I say that is the easiest part. The hardest part is having something to write about that succeeds in drawing words from your inner mind – that is very important, as one can always think of *subjects*, but they have to *matter* in that peculiar way that produces words and some kind of development of thought or theme, or else there's no poem either in thought or words.

Philip Larkin died in 1985 at the age of sixty-three. Ours was a brief encounter and, after his discharge from hospital, I never saw him again. Looking back, his belief that the *Tao Te Ching* was the greatest book ever written must have influenced me subliminally over the years. It suggested the possibility that Chinese thought, if properly translated, can be of interest to other western minds besides that of one brilliant, gifted British poet. It may even have inspired me to base *Watching the Tree* on this very theme.

Of all the ancient Chinese classics, the one which has been most frequently translated into foreign languages is a slim

---

* Author's note: Sir Russell was overweight and used to mumble into his many chins. We, the interns, nicknamed him 'mumble, rumble, neurological jumble'.

volume written 2500 years ago: the *Tao Te Ching* (*Classic of the Tao and Its Virtue*). More than forty different translations in English alone are in print. According to many sources, the author was someone named Lao Zi 老子 (Old Master), a contemporary of Confucius. But some people doubt Lao Zi's existence and think that the book was written by unknown authors in the fourth century BC.

Lao Zi, the founder of Taoism, was born in Ku Xian, Henan province (400 miles south of Beijing) in 571 BC. His real name was Li Er . He came from a distinguished and cultured family and was employed as a curator of the imperial archives and historical documents at the royal court in the capital city of Loyang during the Chou dynasty. Confucius admired him and was said to have sought his advice around 517 BC.

Lao Zi was married and had a son who later became a general in the state of Wei. According to legend, Lao Zi left his post in his old age and travelled west to India, leaving his writing in the hands of a frontier warden guarding the Hankukuan Pass.

His book, the *Tao Te Ching*, is very short. It contains just over 5000 Chinese characters and the entire text will fit on a single sheet of newspaper. Divided into eighty-one separate, tersely worded and rhymed chapters, its concepts are subtle and profound, but its cryptic language lends itself to many different interpretations.

The central theme revolves around the *tao* 道, which means 'the way' or 'the road', but which is often used to indicate the order of Nature. As a philosophy Taoism deals with the unchangeable, eternal and pervasive oneness of the universe; with cycles and the relativity of all standards; and with the return to the divine intelligence of non-being, from which all being has come.

The book begins enigmatically:

> The Tao which can be expressed is not the
>   unchanging Tao;
> The name which can be defined is not the eternal
>   name.

The *tao* is the ancestor of all things. It is powerful but is also invisible and inaudible. It is hidden and nameless *dao ying wu ming* 道隱無名, and operates by non-action (無為 *wu wei*), which means non-interference or letting things take their own spontaneous course: 'Tao takes no action but nothing is left undone.'

Lao Zi's metaphysical concept bears an uncanny resemblance to the teachings of the Dutch philosopher Spinoza (1632–77). Like Lao Zi, Spinoza finds his God in the whole of the universe, which contains all reality. His pantheism essentially restates the same ideas as the *Tao Te Ching*. Rejecting the concept of a personal and emotional God, or one with human attributes who meddles in human affairs, Spinoza envisaged a higher being who acts according to the necessity of His own nature and does not interfere in the everyday life of men. Lao Zi expressed it thus:

> Hence the wise man depends on non-action for
>   action,
> Continues teaching his 'lessons of silence'.
> Yet the multitudinous creatures are influenced by
>   him;
> He does not reject them.
> He nurtures them, but claims no possession of them,
> Oversees them, but does not put pressure on them.
> Accomplishes his purpose, but does not dwell on his
>   achievements,
> And precisely because he calls no attention to his
>   actions
> He is not banished from the completion of his tasks.

In the *Tao Te Ching*, the *tao* is compared to water, which accomplishes much while being meek and receptive. It is all-powerful in its humility. Called by some the 'master of camouflage', Lao Zi taught that power can be disguised as weakness and non-violence will overcome force.

> Nothing under heaven is softer and weaker than
>   water,
> Yet nothing surpasses it in battling the hard and
>   strong.

Like water, the *tao* affects the universe through *wu wei*: a non-invasive and persuasive love whose strengths are its virtue and submission. Lao Zi wrote:

> The best of the best is similar to water.
> Water aids and benefits ten thousand different
>   creatures,
> Yet it neither tussles nor contends,
> But rests content in places despised by others.
> It is this which makes water so near to the Tao.
> Man should consider his home a good dwelling
>   place,
> In his thoughts, he should value the profound,
> In his friendship, he should be gentle and kind,
> In his words, he should be truthful and sincere,
> In his government, he should abide by good order,
> In his affairs, he should be proficient and effective,
> In his actions, he should seize the opportune
>   moment.

Although many of the concepts in the *Tao Te Ching* reach lofty and mystical heights, their effectiveness can be understood and appreciated only through personal transformation. Lao Zi anticipated this problem:

When a scholar of great talent hears the Tao
He tries his best to practice it.
When a scholar of a vorage talent hears the Tao,
He is torn between applying it and not applying it.
When a scholar of inferior talent hears the Tao,
He laughs loudly at it.
If it did not provoke laughter, it would not be the
    Tao.

He wrote of the sense of hidden divine influence in the universe, expressing the mystery and beauty of the *tao* poetically:

Look at it, but one sees nothing,
It is called illusory.
Listen to it, but one hears no sound,
It is called undetectable.
Feel for it, but one touches a void,
It is called minuscule.
These three, because they elude us,
Meld to become one.

At the beginning of the twenty-first century traditional western thought based on Aristotelian logic of the either/or classification is being increasingly challenged by Einstein's theory of relativity. Ironically, 2500 years ago Lao Zi had already written about the rise of relative opposites in his book:

Existence and non-existence are dependent on each
    other
Difficult and easy give rise to the same concept
Long and short are derived by comparison
High differs from low only by position
Sound and echo blend into one harmony
Front and back follow one another in sequence.

In 1927 Werner Heisenberg propounded the Principle of Uncertainty for subatomic particles. 'In the subatomic situation,' he wrote, 'the effects introduced by the observer to observe the phenomenon automatically introduces a degree of uncertainty in the observed phenomenon.' Lao Zi expressed similar sentiments in these words:

> He who knows does not speak;
> He who speaks does not know.

Dualistic thinking in terms of unified opposites was expressed thus:

> Thirty spokes are joined at the nave to build a wheel
> But it is the space between that lets it function
> Lumps of clay are fashioned into a vessel
> But it is the emptiness within that renders it useful
> Doors and windows are cut to build a room
> But it is the enclosure that furnishes a shelter
> As we benefit from that which exists,
> Let us recognise the utility of that which does not.

Lao Zi's intuition about the hidden might of the *tao* is succinctly captured in a few short lines. Without the empty space of the hub in which the wheel turns, the cart cannot move. Without the hollowness in the vessel, the vase has no function. Without the emptiness behind the windows and doors, there is no place to live.

The development of Taoism can be roughly divided into three periods:

- Ancient Period (from 571 BC to 221 BC, when China became united by Qin Shi Huang Di, first emperor of China)

- Middle Period (from 221 BC to AD 906)
- Third Period (from AD 906 to the present).

The wisdom of Lao Zi was supplemented and expanded two centuries after its inception by Zhuang Zi (Master Zuang), who wrote the book also known as *Zhuang Zi*, considered to be one of the most important books of Taoism.

Zhuang Zi was born about 200 years after Lao Zi and died shortly after 300 BC. He was from Mengshien in Henan province (the same province as Lao Zi) and held a minor post as an officer/administrator. In his book he tells us that one day, while he was fishing, two ambassadors from the southern state of Chu came to visit, bringing precious gifts from their ruler. They tried to persuade him to take up the post of prime minister but Zhuang Zi declined without even looking up from his fishing pole.

He was married but childless. When his wife died, his disciples found him sitting on the ground with an inverted basin on his knee. Instead of mourning her, he was singing a song and beating time on the basin, while her coffin lay in a corner awaiting burial. Shocked at his behaviour, they questioned him. This was Zhuang Zi's reply:

'When she died, I was in despair. But soon, I told myself that in death, nothing new has happened. In the beginning, we lacked not only life, but form. Not only form, but spirit. We were blended in one great featureless indistinguishable mass. Then the time arrived when the mass evolved spirit, spirit evolved form and form evolved life.

'Now life in turn has evolved death. Besides nature, man's being also has its seasons; his own sequence of spring and autumn, summer and winter. If someone is tired and lies down to rest, we should not pursue him with cries and laments. I have lost my wife and she has laid down to sleep in the Great Inner Room. To disturb her with my tears would only demonstrate that I am ignorant of the Laws of Nature. That is why I am no longer mourning.'

In another passage Zhuang Zi mused further about death:

How do I know that wanting to be alive is not a great mistake? How do I know that hating to die is not like thinking one has lost one's way, when all the time one is on the path that leads to home? . . .

While a man is dreaming, he does not know that he dreams; nor can he interpret a dream till the dream is done. It is only when he wakes, that he knows it was a dream. Not till the Great Wakening can he know that all this was One Great Dream . . .

He once had a vivid dream in which he was a butterfly fluttering from flower to flower. During the dream he was utterly convinced he was a butterfly. When he woke, he said to himself, 'Am I Zhuang Zi dreaming I was a butterfly or am I a butterfly dreaming of being Zhuang Zi?'

Zhuang Zi developed and refined the basic concepts of the *Tao Te Ching* and taught that the *tao* way is the way of Nature. It includes the substance as well as the manner in which the cosmos exists and acts. Over 2000 years before the birth of Einstein, who propounded that matter and energy are interchangeable, this ancient Chinese sage and his disciples had already suggested that the balance in the universe remains for ever the same. Zhuang Zi conceived of the cosmos as a stream in which one state succeeds another endlessly. Change is the only constant. Time never stops and no state can be retained. There is incessant transformation. However, while everything is changing, for each action there is a reaction so that the cosmic balance remains the same.

When I first started to learn English in earnest, one of the English words that used to puzzle me was 'universe'. The English–Chinese dictionary translated 'universe' into *yu zhou*. The Chinese word *yu* 宇 means 'space'; but *zhou* 宙 means 'infinite time', or 'time without beginning or end'. As teenagers, my third older brother James and I puzzled over the inclusion of 'time' into the concept of 'space' in translating 'universe' into *yu zhou*. A few years later, after James was admitted to Cambridge University in England, he sent me a note. 'According to Einstein's theory of relativity,' he wrote, 'our ancestors were correct all along. Our universe does consist of "space/time" and not space alone. *Yu zhou* is right on the money, after all.'

While doing research for this book, I actually came across the words *yu zhou* in ancient Chinese books. It gave me a thrill to note the similarity between my ancestors' conception of the universe and that of our greatest contemporary physicists.

Zhuang Zi says, 'Tao is real, is faithful, yet does nothing and has no form. Can be handed down, yet cannot be passed from hand to hand. Can be acquired but cannot be seen. Is its own trunk, its own root. Before heaven and earth existed, from the beginning, Tao was there.'

In Taoism, the goal is spiritual freedom, to be achieved in the realm of Nature. Following Nature means *wu wei* (taking no action), through which one will gain contentment, enlightenment and peace. Man should see his lifecycle of birth, growth, decay and death as part of Nature and accept change to be the *tao* of everything in the universe.

During the Middle Period (221 BC–AD 906) Taoism developed more as a religion than a philosophy. The writings of Taoist philosophers such as Lao Zi and Zhuang Zi were carefully culled by priest-magicians to cultivate and reinforce superstitious practices such as the search for immortality and alchemy. Huai Nan Tzu 淮南子 (178–122 BC) first started mixing philosophy with mystical concepts such as spirits and distant fairylands. Certain elements were synthesised by religious leaders and interpreted according to their beliefs. Borrowing from the *I Ching*, they taught that all things were products of cosmic negative and positive forces (*yin* and *yang*), which could be harmonised with the vital force (氣 *qi*) of the universe and concentrated in the human body to promote health and prolong life. They developed breathing techniques (氣功 *qi gong*) in an attempt to control the flow of *qi*, along with special sexual practices which allowed men to regulate and preserve the flow of their semen, thought to be linked to male (*yang*) *qi*. Various 'scriptures' were written which aimed to provide Taoism with a theory as well as an elaborate system of practice. Ceremonies were formulated and names given to a great number of gods: kitchen; stars; ancestors; famous historical personages; literature; medicine; wealth; immortals; ideals, and countless others. Taoists had their own clergy, temples and images. The head of the clergy was called the Heavenly Father, a title retained by his direct descendants. Taoism became an organised religion as well as a state cult, reaching the zenith of its power and influence during the Tang dynasty (AD 618–960), partly because the Tang emperor had the same surname as Lao Zi (Li).

Over the years Taoism, Confucianism and Buddhism imitated, influenced and intermingled with each other extensively. One of the most popular Taoist gods, Guan Yin 觀音 (Goddess of Mercy), was borrowed wholesale from Buddhism. Another was a courageous and red-faced military hero named Guan

41

Yu 關羽, who fought and died during the Three Kingdoms War (AD 220–264). However, Taoism was less organised than Buddhism and lacked an intellectually enlightened leadership; it gradually widened its sphere and lost its focus. Primary objectives became earthly blessings such as wealth, happiness, health, children, longevity and the fulfilment of personal desires. These were to be obtained through witch-craft, magic, aphrodisiacs and incantations. Instead of developing a comprehensive philosophy based on the *Tao Te Ching*, Taoists concentrated on cultivating practices such as breath control (*qi gong*), periodic vegetarianism, meditation, shadow-boxing (太極 *tai chi* – modelled on the movements of animals such as birds and panthers), and attempts to trans-form mercury into gold. Geomancy (*feng shui* 風水), fortune-telling, divination and the use of charms were some of the offshoots of religious Taoism. Ritual observances became increasingly 'practical'. Food was offered to departed ances-tors but eaten after the ceremony by living relatives. A west-erner summed it all up by saying that in China the intellectuals questioned everything and believed in nothing whereas the uneducated questioned nothing and believed in everything.

With the coming of Christianity and western missionaries following the Opium War in the nineteenth century, Taoism as an organised religion declined and faded away. However, its influence is deeply etched in the Chinese psyche. Many Taoist temples, gods, legends, fairy-tales, ceremonies, festivals and traditions have not only survived but are still celebrated in China as well as in Chinatowns all over the world. In addition, the teachings of Lao Zi and Zhuang Zi have left to Chinese thought their lasting legacy of agnosticism, scepti-cism, tolerance and detachment.

4

Do Not Do to Others What You Do Not Wish Others to Do to You

己所不欲，勿施於人

JI SUO BU YU, WU SHI YU REN

The earliest act of filial piety I ever witnessed involved my father. My grandmother (Nai Nai) was still alive and I must have been about four. A French relative of my stepmother, Niang, had given her a beautiful red and gold tin of expensive imported bonbons. Each chocolate was wrapped in silver foil and studded with bits of crunchy nut. After dinner Niang opened her gift and showed off the tempting sweets. However, she presented a candy to each of the grown-ups only.

As we five stepchildren salivated, she closed the lid with a final snap of her wrist. 'I'm afraid there isn't enough to pass around,' she announced. 'These chocolates are very special and came from Belgium. They are made with the best eggs, butter, sugar, chocolate and nuts. My brother-in-law had to stand in line for twenty minutes at Kiessling's to buy them. Now they're already sold out. I must reserve the rest for your father's important guests. You children are not to touch them, do you hear? Otherwise your father and I will be very angry.'

We nodded but our eyes lingered longingly on the sparkling box. Big Brother (Gregory), who was Nai Nai's favourite, ran over to her and begged in a whisper to have a tiny little bite of hers. She could never resist him and even though the chocolate was halfway into her mouth, she bit off a piece and gave it to him. Big Brother then picked up the wrapper and licked it clean.

That night I was awakened from a deep sleep by loud voices from downstairs. I crept out of bed and stood by the banisters to watch. Second Older Brother (Edgar) was cowering between Nai Nai and Father on the landing below and sobbing uncontrollably. He was dressed in pyjamas and his face was covered with blood. From their conversation, I gathered that Second Brother had got up in the middle of the night to help himself to the forbidden sweets. Niang surprised him in the act and summoned Father, who rushed down and caught him trying to escape. In his anger, Father slapped Second Brother so hard that he caused a tear in his scalp with his ring.

Hearing Second Brother's cries, Nai Nai had tottered down in her small, bound feet to protect him. 'Stop it! Stop it!' I heard Nai Nai shout in her quavering voice. 'How *dare* you go on beating him when I ordered you to stop?! Just because he took some candy! Look at all the blood! Are you trying to kill him? Why don't you kill me first?'

There was a short silence. Father hung his head.

'Don't you remember the words of Confucius?' Nai Nai continued. 'The body and hair and skin are received from your parents and may not be harmed. Here you are, beating your own son almost to death because of a few chocolates. If you didn't want him to be tempted, why were the sweets shown to him in the first place? When you were growing up, did anyone ever beat you like that?

'You heard me ordering you to stop as I came down the stairs and you still went on! How *dare* you! You are an unfilial son to disobey me! Kneel down! Kneel down and apologise! Remember the words of Confucius! Being unfilial is the worst crime!'

Then I saw my father fall slowly to his knees in submission to my grandmother.

For over 2000 years Confucius had a greater influence on China than any other individual. He was a philosopher, not a prophet, and Confucianism was a way of life, not a religion. His word was law and a quote from Confucius ended all arguments. He taught that *xiao* 孝 (translated as 'filial piety') was the root of virtue and the origin of culture. A more accurate description of *xiao* is 'filial devotion' or 'the dominance of elders in the relationship between parents and children'. Morality in China was based on this singularly Confucian concept.

Confucius was born in 551 BC in the state of Lu, which is now the province of Shandong in north-eastern China. His surname was Kung 孔. The name Confucius is a latinised version of 'Grand Master Kung' (孔夫子 Kung Fu Zi). Confucius' father died three years after his birth and he was brought up by his impoverished mother. Though he was from a noble and educated family, he was without rank and made his living as a book-keeper, working for the government. He was married and had children. *The Analects*, a book of his sayings written by his disciples, reveals the living Confucius as a fussy and demanding man. When food was mushy or not cooked according to his taste, he refused to eat. When ginger was used to flavour his food, he refused to eat. When rice was spoilt by heat or damp, he refused to eat. When vegetables were not in season, he refused to eat. When meat was not sliced properly or a dish served without its proper sauce, he refused to eat. When wine or shredded meat were purchased ready-made from the market, he refused to eat. Rice could never be white enough and minced meat could never be chopped fine enough. Consequently, according to his students, he did not eat much, and after some years his wife left him.

By all accounts, he was athletic and adept in sports such as archery, hunting, fishing, driving chariots and riding. He had a passionate temperament and described himself as 'a person who forgets to eat if he is enthusiastic about a project; someone who becomes unaware of worries or the approach of old age when happy.' Once, after listening to a piece of music, he was so overcome that, for three months, he could not taste meat, saying, 'I never thought music could be so beautiful.'

During his life China was only nominally united under the royal house of Chou (1122–256 BC). The various states were in effect miniature kingdoms, each with its own ruler, court, bureaucracy and army. The kings fought battles against each other almost as a past-time, while oppressing and mercilessly taxing their subjects to finance their wars.

Distressed by the misery and chaos, Confucius resigned his post and spent the next fifteen years teaching. Gradually, a group of young men gathered around him and became his disciples. He studied the character of each and sought to develop the total man by teaching him how to think and find answers for himself. He conversed with his students and these dialogues were recorded by them in *The Analects*. Of his followers, more than half were ultimately successful in obtaining government posts in different states.

In his dialogues, whenever Confucius used the word

'world', he meant the Chinese world. When he used the term *jun zi* 君子 (ideal person), he meant men and not women. He was a misogynist and treated women as second-class citizens who should stay home and perform household chores. Once he declared that 'only uneducated women were virtuous'. On another occasion he identified females as 'little people' (小人 *xiao ren*), suggesting that the two were similar.

At the age of fifty Confucius was given a high post in the government of his native state of Lu, supposedly as the Minister of Justice and Assistant Minister of Public Works. However, it was a ceremonial post without authority and he was unable to put any of his ideas into practice. After four years he resigned in disgust and spent the next thirteen travelling from state to state in search of an enlightened ruler who would appoint him as chief administrator. He was imbued with the belief that he had a 'heavenly mission' to carry out political and social reforms. However, no ruler would employ him, and he spent the last five years of his life teaching in his home state of Lu until his death in 479 BC at the age of seventy-three.

Confucius seldom spoke of the supernatural; nor did he seem to worry about the immortality of his soul. However, he did not deny the existence of spirits or the possibility of life after death. When asked directly, he replied, 'When one does not understand life, how can one understand death?' Elsewhere he said, 'Offer sacrifices to the spirits as if the spirits are present . . . Respect the spirits, but keep them at a distance.'

Confucius advocated a doctrine of practical common sense which attempted to create order and harmony in the society of his era. His sayings stayed close to home and wrestled with human life and human problems. In short, he was not a prophet but China's first educator and foremost sociologist.

Confucianism was welcomed by dynastic rulers through-out China's long history because it viewed the state as a big family headed by the emperor, who was like a benevolent father, constantly devoted to his people's welfare. Confucius taught that all territory and all citizens belonged to the sovereign, whose right to rule was given by the Mandate of Heaven. Though the emperor's power was absolute, he was to rule by moral example and not by force. A ruler who failed to live up to the Mandate of Heaven because of personal amorality and corruption should abdicate in favour of a virtuous man; if necessary he should be overthrown by revolution.

Confucius listed five cardinal relationships in society: between ruler and minister; father and son; husband and wife; older brother and younger brother; friend and friend. Of these, only the relationship between friends is equal.

As a corollary of the five cardinal human relationships, he expounded the doctrine of social status, giving every person his 'proper place' in society. The term *li* 禮 may be defined as a combination of etiquette, propriety and correct naming. A person's name and title denoted a social code, an attitude and a mental background. An emperor must be a true emperor. No emperor deserves to be called an emperor unless he fulfils his function. No father should be called a father unless he acts like one. Reality and function, name and actuality, must correspond. So must action and words. The minister must kowtow in front of his emperor. A son must show respect and gratitude towards his father. Social obligations between people in China necessitate certain codes of behaviour, which in turn provide order and stability.

In the 1940s, during my early childhood, Tianjin was ruled by the Japanese and the French. Although my grandfather loathed these foreigners, he was always respectful and law-abiding towards them. Once he prevented a youthful employee from sticking nails into the tyre of a Japanese army officer's car. 'It is Heaven's will that we are governed by these loathsome creatures,' he said. 'We must accept our fate and adapt. When the right time comes, a new ruler will arrive.' This type of Confucian logic probably explains why an enormous country like China could be dominated by handfuls of westerners for over 100 years. When Japan lost the Second World War, my grandfather treated officials from Chiang Kai-shek's government with the same obedience. Later on, in Hong Kong, he was equally deferential to the British colonialists.

Another important Chinese term is *min fen* 名份 or 'duty accorded by name'. In Chinese families, children (or relatives) are not called by their given names but by names corresponding to their place in the family. The oldest son is called Big Brother, the second son Second Brother, and so on. There are separate Chinese words for 'older brother' (哥 *ge*) and 'younger brother' (弟 *di*); 'older sister' (姐 *jie*) and 'younger sister' (妹 *mei*). The younger brother (or sister) is expected to listen to and obey the older brother (or sister) so that order can be preserved in the family. At home, we younger children called our oldest brother Big Brother (大哥 Da Ge). My oldest sister, who was one year older than Big Brother, called him Da Di 大弟 (Big Younger Brother). However, when a member of the older generation such as our parents, grandparents, uncles and aunts called him Da Di, the words took on the meaning of 'oldest son'. This type of nomenclature provided a clear and unequivocal social stratification which defined a person's status in his family.

I never cared for my sister Lydia. As the oldest of seven children in our family, she was known to us as Da Jie 大姐 (Big Sister). She was often put in charge and would flaunt her authority. When I was little, she hectored me mercilessly and often beat me.

After a long separation we met each other again. By then, a reversal of fortune had taken place. I was no longer the despised little sister whom she could bully at will but a successful physician practising in America. She, meanwhile, had been stuck in a loveless marriage in Communist China for thirty years. Although I was shocked by her downtrodden appearance and humble demeanour, all the familiar emotions of respect and fear re-emerged as soon as she uttered my childhood name, Wu Mei 五妹 (Fifth Younger Sister). Suddenly, I reverted to my former status. Respectfully, I called her Da Jie and dutifully agreed to do everything she asked. I did not trust her but was eager to please and felt compelled to help her although I could not understand why. I knew my sister was ruthless but not once did I consider refusing her. Perhaps my mind was so conditioned by Confucian concepts of *min fen* that I could no longer think for myself.

The word *xiao* has no true equivalent in the English language. Confucius considered *xiao*, or filial piety, to be life's most important virtue and the origin of Chinese culture. In the *Classic of Filial Piety* he said, 'The *jun zi* (ideal person) teaches filial piety so that man may respect all the fathers in the world. He teaches brotherliness so that younger brothers may respect older brothers in the world. He teaches duty to the subject so that subjects will respect all who are rulers in the world.' Morality and *li* (etiquette) in the family, he hoped, would be disseminated outside the family to become the foundation for morality and *li* in general so that people might live together in peace and harmony: 'Peace in the state begins with order in the family . . . The people who love and respect their parents would never dare show hatred and disrespect to others.'

As my grandmother told my father that night in Tianjin,

> The body and hair and skin are received from the parents and may not be injured: this is the beginning of filial piety. To do the right thing and walk according to the right morals, thus leaving a good name in posterity, in order to glorify one's ancestors, this is the culmination of filial piety. Filial piety begins with serving one's parents, leads to serving one's king and ends in establishing one's character.

A person could not be good to anyone else unless he was first good to his parents. Family was the bridge between the individual and society. A family should be held together not only by blood, property and shared responsibilities; but also by common ideals such as love of virtue and honour as well as earthly goals such as wealth, success, longevity, many sons and happiness.

My grandfather once showed me a schoolbook from his own childhood in the 1880s. He told me that it had been written during the Song dynasty (960–1271); the same text had been taught to Chinese children for over 750 years. The author had adapted the teachings of Confucius specially for children and mapped out a life plan for them based on filial piety.

When my siblings and I were growing up in China, we

younger generation invariably treated our elders with deference. Age was honoured to such a degree that it was not unusual for my grandfather and his generation to add a few years to their chronological age when asked. At Chinese New Year my brothers and I used to kneel before our parents to wish them happiness and longevity. We continued to do so even after our graduation from British universities. This custom was known as *bai nian* 拜年: *bai* means 'to worship or do obeisance'; *nian* means 'year'.

These rites and rituals reinforced the concept of filial piety so effectively that I don't remember any of us uttering a single disrespectful remark to our parents' face. Instead, we were fearful and obedient and our lives were focused on pleasing our unloving parents. We never dared complain, even when unjustly punished. We also accepted blindly what our parents decided for us.

Filial piety dictated that my oldest sister Lydia should remain silent when our parents ordered her to leave school and enter an arranged marriage at the age of seventeen. After graduating from Cambridge University, my brother James was ordered back to Hong Kong to work at Father's side and did so for a meagre salary even though he was inundated with offers from other firms. Louise Lam was introduced to him by our stepmother as his prospective bride and he dutifully married her. I myself turned down a job as assistant lecturer in the department of medicine at Hong Kong University Medical School to be an intern at a government hospital in order to please my parents.

Confucius thought that religion should exist for the purpose of education and moral cultivation. He did not believe in divi-

nation, fortune-telling, or conjectures concerning Heaven and Hell; his approach was much more pragmatic and rational. To him, the *tao* or Heaven stood for a positive, just force in the universe. It was the source of truth, goodness and moral law. Good and evil deeds would bring their own consequences.

He advised men to direct their own destiny, rather than resorting to a fatalistic reliance on spirits. He promoted ceremonies and rites to worship Heaven, honour the ancestors and commemorate great men. Expressions of respect towards ancestors and great men should not end with their death: ancestor-worship was merely the continuation of a human relationship. Immortality was to be obtained through an individual's own endeavours, through virtue and wisdom.

In Confucian (as well as Chinese) thought the word *tian* 天, translated as 'Heaven', means much more than the sky above. Because the word God does not exist in the Chinese language, the term *tian* encompasses all the following concepts relating to God: supreme being; prime mover; divine light; the *tao;* ultimate reality and many other synonyms. As with other expressions concerning religion, *tian*'s interpretation depends on one's personal convictions. The exact definition of the Chinese word *tian* became the focal point of the Rites controversy, a bitter quarrel between the Jesuits and other orders of the Catholic Church that began in seventeenth-century China and lasted for nearly two hundred years. It was a metaphysical dispute involving the didactic question of whether the concept of God and Heaven should conform only to that taught by the Catholic Church. Were Chinese rituals of ancestor-worship and the cult of Confucius idolatrous practices or were they social occasions to pay respect to one's elders? Was the Chinese idea of Heaven (*tian*) spiritual or material? Did the term *tian* mean 'dweller of Heaven' as well as 'Heaven'?

My grandfather was very open-minded about religion. He professed himself a Buddhist but often read my father's copy of the Bible in Chinese. Once he told me there was no contradiction between Confucianism, Buddhism and Christianity. All three preached similar concepts.

'It's all a question of viewpoint,' he said. 'The Christians believe in Jesus whereas Confucius believed in *jun zi* (the ideal man). The priests talk of rewards in Heaven after death. Confucius taught us to concentrate on being a good person on earth. Why can't a person be a Confucian, a Buddhist, a Catholic and a Protestant at the same time? Why does one belief have to exclude another? After all, they all teach the same principles.'

Further comparing the teachings of Jesus to that of Confucius, he continued, 'The Christian idea of charity is the same as our Confucian concept of *jen* 仁 (benevolent concern for one's fellow men). Christian charity means love and justice. This is exactly what Confucius meant when he said, "Virtue is to love man and wisdom is to understand man." Both taught the principle of reciprocity: "*Ji suo bu yu, wu shi yu ren*" (Do not do to others what you do not wish others to do to you). Both condemned force as a way of life and frowned upon profit or advantage as the only standards of value.

'Instead of the Ten Commandments, we Chinese try to live by the ethical code contained in the *tao* and attempt to become an ideal person of noble character with honour and integrity.

'The Christians believe in life after death, whereas we Chinese Buddhists believe in reincarnation. The main difference seems to be our concept of *xiao* (filial piety) and our belief that our ancestors' spirits remain active and exert beneficial influences on our behalf.'

Confucian beliefs were revolutionary when they were first propounded because *jun zi* originally meant a member of the social elite – someone who had been born into the aristocracy. But according to Confucius, any man whose conduct and character warranted it might become a *jun zi* regardless of his ancestry. He emphasised the obligations rather than the rights of individuals. The adoption of the teachings of Confucius during the Han dynasty (202 BC–AD 221) led to the eventual downfall of feudalism in China and the emergence of a more classless society. Every man was given the opportunity to rise in the world through education. Titles and ranks were now determined by ability and not by heredity. Confucius emphasised individual worth; he thought that anyone should be able to become a sage. Nobility was based on merit, not birth. 'In learning,' said Confucius, 'there should be no class distinction.'

He advised kings to hand authority over to their ministers: 'Kings should reign but not rule.' The government should be administered by the most talented and capable men in the nation, carefully chosen for their character, education and ability. Ministers should be sincere, incorruptible and rule by moral example. A good government should aim to bring about the well-being and happiness of the people because all men desire happiness. Humanity could only find happiness if the nation existed as a cooperative community of free men.

Confucius believed that force must be made subordinate to the power of justice and used only as a last resort. Soldiers could only fight effectively if they were convinced of the justice of the cause they were fighting for. A soldier's morale depended on his moral conviction and Confucius advised his students to become not men of the sword but men of moral nobility; not fighters but scholar gentlemen. This is in striking contrast to the Japanese ideal of *bushido* or the Way of the

Warrior, and the samurai notions of fighting to the death, along with a fanatical loyalty to the emperor.

Matteo Ricci, the Italian Jesuit priest who was a missionary in China for twenty years and died in 1610 in Beijing, was awestruck by the 'scholar-philosophers' who held power in the China of the Ming dynasty.

> The entire kingdom is administered by the Order of the Learned, commonly known as the Philosophers. The responsibility for orderly management of the entire realm is wholly and completely committed to their care. The army, both officers and soldiers, hold them in high respect and show them the promptest obedience and deference, and not infrequently the military are disciplined by them as a schoolboy might be punished by his master . . . The Philosophers far excel military leaders in the good will and respect of the people and in opportunities of acquiring wealth. What is still more surprising to strangers is that these same Philosophers, as they are called, with respect to nobility of sentiment and in contempt of danger and death, where fidelity to King and country is concerned, surpass even those whose particular profession is the defence of the fatherland.

Besides cultivating the intellect and imparting knowledge, the purpose of education was also to discipline a student's morals and emotions, as well as to train his character and develop leadership potential. Confucius pointed out the way and asked questions, expecting his disciples to find their own answers. He taught with tireless zeal (誨人不倦 *hui ren bu juan*) and dreamt of an enlightened citizenry and universal education based on intellectual democracy.

He had a strong sense of history and looked to ancient sages as models. He frequently referred to the past in discussions with his disciples: the study of history, he thought, would show them how moral principles could be extrapolated from historical events. Goodness would lead to happiness, prosperity and peace; whereas evil would invite suffering and chaos.

Perhaps because of the influence of Confucius, history has been taken very seriously in China for the last 2000 years. Great men and events of the past have provided endless fascination and founts of material for the scholars, story-tellers, novelists, dramatists, poets and painters who came later. Since the time of the great historian Si Ma Qian 司馬遷 (145–90 BC), who wrote his seminal book *Shi Ji* 史記 (*Historical Record*) while incarcerated in a prison cell, emperors have employed salaried bureaucrats to record the daily happenings of their reign. These writers were paid to fulfil a function and their writing reflected this. They often concealed evil deeds and whitewashed defeats.

These records were then edited into two versions: a national history of the current dynasty, which of necessity was a list of citations joined by platitudes and cliché-ridden flattery; and a standard history of the previous dynasty, which was more objective and accurate. The Chinese emperors believed that the history of a dynasty should be compiled in its entirety and made public only by the dynasty following it. Lu Qi, a third-century writer and critic, described such historical records as 'the enclosure of boundless space in a square foot of paper'.

During the Song dynasty the prominent scholar-philosopher Zhu Xi (1130–1200) selected four books from the Confucian Classics to form the basic texts for the imperial civil service examinations. These four books (*si shu* 四書) exerted enormous influence in China until the examinations were abolished in 1905.

Under this examination system the process of book-learning acquired astronomical prestige. Every scrap of paper with written words on it was treated with respect.

My grandfather told me that in his youth, large boxes, painted red, were placed at street corners as receptacles for scraps of waste paper covered with writing of any sort. Four gilded characters (*jing xi zi zhi* 敬惜字紙 – 'respect and cherish words') were painted on the boxes. Men with bamboo rods and baskets patrolled the streets to pick up any stray pieces of paper with writing. The contents of the receptacles were gathered together by successful examination candidates at regular intervals and burnt at a special shrine in the Temple of Confucius. Music was played during the ceremony while the scholars prostrated themselves in worship.

Confucian ideals and the emphasis on education became ingrained in the consciousness of the populace. Only through scholarship could a man gain access to power and wealth. Even today, a century after the abrogation of the imperial examinations, their legacy and prestige survive in the imaginations of people influenced by Confucianism (Chinese, Japanese, Korean or otherwise), no matter where they may be in the world. In many Chinese minds, an educated person, no matter how poor, still commands more respect than one who is rich and ignorant.

The happiest memories of my miserable childhood in Shanghai are linked to my education. Coming home to my Aunt Baba, my father's spinster sister with whom I shared a room, and presenting her with a report card studded with As was the highlight of my existence. I loved to see the look of joyful pride in her eyes. She used to lock my good report cards in a safe deposit box, which she kept hidden in her closet, and wear the key on a gold chain around her neck, as if my grades were also some precious jewel impossible to replace. Once she said to me, 'These cards are worth more to me than all the diamonds in the world. Mark my words, if you study hard, anything is possible! You can be anything you set your mind to be.'

I never forgot her words.

Although Confucius died in relative obscurity as a failed would-be politician, his ideas gained increasing renown throughout China after his death. From 140 BC (Han dynasty) until 1905 all educational, professional and political advancement was based on a man's knowledge of the Confucian classics. Society was divided into four classes, in the following order of importance: the scholars (*shi* 士), the farmers (*nong* 農), the artisans (*gong* 工) and the merchants (*shang* 商). During the Tang dynasty (618–906) an unprecedented and unique Chinese institution was initiated which was to last for the next 1200 years: the annual imperial civil examinations, which were overseen by the government. This was a sort of national IQ or scholastic aptitude test based on the memorisation and interpretation of the Confucian classics. The stakes were enormous. Regardless of his birth, background, age, temperament or appearance, a man could leap from rags to riches overnight if he managed to pass the three sets of examinations. Anyone could rise in society. By the 1890s (Qing dynasty) over 2,000,000 candidates were sitting the test every year.

The first set was held at the district level. Those who passed were awarded the title of *xiu cai* 秀才 (budding talent). Though still commoners and ineligible for government service, they were now exempt from the labour tax. They were also excused from official labour and corporal punishment by flogging. Considered 'intellectuals' in their villages, many were supported by municipal foundations and treated with special consideration. Their average age was twenty-four.

The second exam was held at the provincial level and led to the degree of *ju ren* 舉人 (recommended man). The successful students were more valued in society. Now qualified to hold minor official positions, they were no longer commoners, and were permitted to wear distinctive clothing as well as gold buttons on their hats. Their average age was thirty.

Success in the third exam led to the degree of *jin shi* 進士 (admitted scholar). Eligible now to be appointed officials of the middle rank, such as a district magistrate or assistant secretary, these scholars also qualified for admission to the imperial palace to sit the final examination. The best candidates from the palace progressed to the Hanlin Academy, where the highest mandarins were trained. Their average age was thirty-five or over.

The top graduate of the academy was called *zhuang yuan* 狀元 (the very best). He would be personally decorated by the emperor and paraded through the capital on a white horse as the cleverest man in China. He would be appointed as a mandarin of the highest rank, and might even be 'awarded' a royal princess as his bride.

Thus, the opportunity existed in China for every village schoolboy to rise in the world through education. By studying hard, anyone could excel. The new nobility in China were those who graduated from the Hanlin Academy. Children of mandarins did not automatically inherit their fathers' titles.

They had to sit the exam like any ordinary peasant or labourer.

For over 2000 years Chinese emperors canonised Confucius and promoted his teachings. Though China was conquered by the Mongols during the Yuan dynasty (1277–1367) and the Manchus during the Qing dynasty (1644–1911), the civil examination system was maintained and the syllabus remained unchanged. In fact, the foreign invaders seem to have immersed themselves in Confucian culture and some of them (such as the eighteenth-century Manchu emperor Qian Long 乾隆) became more Confucian than the Chinese.

The cohesion and historical continuity of such a vast and populous country (in contrast to the myriad small nations of Europe) may have come about partly because China had a common written language. But the fact that the ideals of Confucius continued to be taught for two millennia probably played an equally seminal role. Communication is the key to the development of any country's political, cultural and linguistic unity. The Chinese communicated with each other not only through a shared, standard, written language but, more importantly, through a shared, common world view based on Confucianism.

Matteo Ricci was amazed when he came across this singularly Chinese educational system. He considered it a matchless way to provide the country with an efficient, learned and enlightened bureaucracy. However, there were some serious, long-lasting and far-reaching negative consequences to this educational meritocracy undreamt of by Confucius, Ricci or anyone else.

Throughout China, education became limited to the study of the works of Confucius because passing the imperial examinations was the only method of advancement. A whole system was built around this goal. There were private tutors, village and town schools, as well as colleges and government scholarships. Study consisted of memorisation and endless interpretation of the classics. This led to the mechanical shuffling of words rather than any development of new ideas. It stifled creativity, critical thinking and intellectual curiosity. Confucian sayings were accepted as sacred and accurate on every subject. Originality was feared and change condemned as heresy.

From the Tang dynasty on, the emperors used the imperial civil examination system to 'brain-wash' and control the minds of the best and brightest of China. Since the average student spent twenty years preparing for the examinations, he had little time or inclination to develop dangerous and seditious thoughts of rebellion. The system provided the nation with a loyal bureaucracy. Meanwhile the scholars also became enslaved by their long years of drudgery. They began to think alike and dared not venture into new intellectual realms.

All other fields of study were considered to be a waste of time because they did not carry any weight in the examinations. Hence there was no development of mathematics, physics, chemistry or biology. This may have been one of the reasons why China fell behind the west in science and technology: astronomy became astrology and medicine veered into necromancy and black magic. According to Matteo Ricci, in sixteenth-century China

The study of mathematics and that of medicine are held in low esteem, because they are not fostered by honours as is the study of philosophy, to which students are attracted by the hope of the glory and rewards attached to it. This may readily be seen in the interest taken in the study of moral philosophy. The man who is promoted to the higher degrees in this field prides himself in the fact that he has in truth attained to the pinnacle of Chinese happiness.

However, Confucian studies were so boring and abstruse that many people had no desire to become a Confucian scholar. Since the only purpose of literacy was to pass the imperial civil examinations, most farmers and labourers did not even bother to learn to read and write.

Besides being terse, archaic, devoid of punctuation, esoteric and full of ambiguity, classic Chinese was a dead language. Nobody has spoken it since the time of Confucius; it has only been read and studied. Many of the words had been obsolete for hundreds, if not thousands of years. As time went on, this discrepancy between the literary language of Confucius and the spoken language of the day became greater and greater. Yet education meant learning by heart the works of Confucius and passing the imperial civil examinations. After years of study, students who failed the examinations were unfit to do anything except become teachers of Confucian thought or professional letter-writers. In addition, these failed scholars tended to see themselves as the educated elite, and considered any work (in commerce or commodities, for instance) to be beneath them. Though frequently unable to make a living, they nevertheless felt vastly superior to the 'uneducated' and illiterate farmers and labourers around them. This led to mutual resentment and widespread discontent among the 'workers', who considered the unemployed scholars 'lazy parasites'.

Trained in ancient classical Chinese, many scholars were unable even to write a modern report or business note. Not only were they incapable of writing in 'modern' Chinese; they thought it beneath their dignity to do so, considering the practice unliterary and frivolous.

However, in order to capture the mood and emotions of human beings in identifiable situations, prose has to be written in a living language. To make characters come alive, words must capture the poetry, passion, anguish, laughter, pathos and grandeur of men speaking to each other in the everyday vernacular. This meant that, over the centuries, very few great Chinese novels were written.

Composing fiction in the spoken language was considered despicable by the literati. The word 'novel' in Chinese is known as *xiao shuo* 小説 (little talk). Serious examination candidates about to become pillars of the establishment simply did not stoop to write anything so trivial. Instead, such frivolous creations were composed in secret behind closed doors by scholars who were considered a little peculiar. The authors themselves were often ashamed of their novels and would deny authorship when questioned. Intellectual snobbery and misogyny may have been two important reasons for the absence of a Chinese Shakespeare or Jane Austen in imperial China.

In 1917 Dr Hu Shih 胡適博士 (1891–1962), then working at Columbia University in New York, finally proposed that the everyday language as spoken by the people should be the literary medium of twentieth-century Chinese prose. Dr Hu was eventually successful in revolutionising and liberating Chinese language from the stylised, cliché-ridden, ancient prose of Confucius. From then on, Chinese essays and novels were written in the same language as the thoughts which occupied the writer's mind.

Another negative consequence of the wholesale adoption of Confucianism was the acceptance of women's inferior status. Confucius was a misogynist and, for over 2000 years, women were treated as hand-maidens to men. 'Between husband and wife, there should be attention to their separate functions,' he said. Unfortunately, 'separate functions' meant two distinct classes. Men were the bread-winners who worked outside the home and controlled the purse-strings. Women were kept inside the house and served husband and family. They were second-class citizens and were not encouraged to read or write because Confucius had also proclaimed that 'only uneducated women were virtuous'.

A man could have more than one wife. He could also divorce his wife and remarry at any time. A woman, however, was required to remain chaste under all circumstances and swear complete loyalty to her husband at all times, whether he was alive or dead. When a woman was young, she obeyed her father. When she married, she obeyed her husband. When she was widowed, she obeyed her son.

Apart from her dowry and gifts from her husband, a woman possessed no money or income. When parents died, land and property were given only to the sons. In the New Territories of prosperous Hong Kong, this practice is still going on.

In the official histories of the dynasties kept by the emperors, a special section was reserved to commemorate exemplary deeds performed by great women. These records were woefully short of examples of women who had demonstrated any intellectual accomplishments but were full of widows who had killed themselves to guard their chastity. One dowager in the Tang dynasty (ninth century AD) was so incensed at having her arm dragged by a male innkeeper that she cut it off. She was much praised and made the 'list' in the official histories. During the Song dynasty (960–1276) it was considered a moral crime for widows to remarry. Some committed suicide at their husband's funeral. A widow in the Yuan dynasty (1277–1367) was honoured for refusing to undress and show her doctor her diseased breast, eventually dying of her malady. Thus, self-mutilation (or suicide) by widows who guarded their chastity for the sake of their dead husbands was considered to be a sign of the highest virtue. Thus were women encouraged to 'distinguish' themselves and 'make a name' for posterity.

The barbaric custom of foot-binding started during the Tang dynasty and continued for 1200 years. The craze for small feet started in the court of an emperor whose daughter had club feet and loved to dance. Soon, a group of women dancers were binding their feet to perform a famous dance called the Golden Lotus. The custom spread and mothers began to bind their daughters' feet from a young age. My grandmother was only three years old when her feet were bound. The smallest feet measured not more than three inches and girls were crippled for life in order to be marriageable. The sight of small feet was supposed to arouse erotic feelings in Chinese men and many love poems were written in praise of them.

Parents routinely favoured their sons and discriminated against their daughters. Unwanted infant daughters were murdered, abandoned or sold. Even today, most of the infants put up for adoption by Chinese orphanages in mainland China are female.

Discrimination against women was almost ingrained into the thinking of Chinese men of my father's generation. When I visited my Aunt Baba in Shanghai in 1979, she introduced me to her attorney, a dapper little man who suffered from terrible arthritis of the hip. On our way out to dinner he hobbled along the pavement with the aid of a stout walking stick, huffing and puffing all the way. In those days few Shanghai homes possessed washers or dryers. Bamboo poles poked out of many windows carrying sheets, towels, underwear, blouses and Mao jackets. I noticed the attorney painfully going out of his way to avoid walking under the poles laden with clothes and tried to reassure him: 'Don't worry. Nothing will drip on you. It all looks very dry.'

'I know,' he replied. 'Sorry to delay you but I just hate walking under a pole carrying women's clothes. My parents told me I wouldn't grow if I ever walked under a pair of woman's underpants.'

This from the lips of a graduate of Shanghai's prestigious St John's University who was approaching eighty years of age!

Confucius also taught the negation of self for the good of the family. Obligations towards one's parents took precedence over individual desires. The notion of 'family' is deeply ingrained in the Chinese psyche. The word 'country' is translated into *jia xiang* 家鄉 (family village), *zu guo* 祖國 (ancestor nation), or *guo jia* 國家 (nation family). These are solid, concrete, emotional, gut-wrenching words which appeal to Chinese instincts because the concept of 'family' is incorporated in them. Confucius said, 'Peace in the state begins with order in the family.'

At best, these beliefs led to family unity, self-sacrifice, self-control, loyalty, duty, respect and gratitude for one's elders, and a sense of family honour. At worst, however, this emphasis on family values deteriorated into selfishness and a lack of social consciousness.

As I write, I have a photograph in front of me of a line of American tourists taken at the Great Wall of China in January

1980. We were queuing up in the freezing cold to use the public toilets, which were filthy. We had been forewarned of the appalling conditions awaiting us and had rolled up the legs of our trousers in anticipation.

Inside, there was an atrocious stink and no toilet paper. The lavatory had no seat and the rim was so filthy that many refused to sit down but squatted above it instead. Its chain had broken and flushing was impossible. A thick layer of excreta swarming with flies lay at the bottom of the bowl. The floor around the toilet was wet and stinky with slime. The reason for the rolled-up trouser legs was to prevent them from being soiled when we pulled them down to relieve ourselves.

Later on we visited the home of my Chinese relative, who lived nearby. Though her apartment was small and spartan, every room was neat and clean. We asked to use her bathroom and recounted our experience at the Great Wall. She laughed and shrugged. 'What do you expect? Those are public toilets. Why should anyone take care of them?'

This lack of social consciousness manifests itself in scores of other ways: the indiscriminate dumping of trash, environmental pollution, corruption, nepotism, favouritism and diversion of public funds to benefit one's own family. Discoveries in medicine and science were regarded as family secrets that should be neither revealed nor shared, no matter how beneficial they were to mankind at large. Occasionally, these skills were taught to a favourite son, but often they died with their inventors.

In the 1940s, on my way to school in Shanghai I often saw infants wrapped in newspapers left in doorways to die. Pedestrians used to hurry by without a backward glance. A well-known Chinese aphorism says, 'One should sweep the snow in front of one's own door and not be concerned with the frost on one's neighbour's roof.'

Drivers on the streets of Chinese cities experience this at first hand. Changing lanes and cutting into moving traffic are life-threatening manoeuvres in Shanghai, Hong Kong or Taipei. One of my English friends calls it 'cut-throat driving'. There is no such thing as 'road courtesy'. However, if the traffic policeman knows your cab-driver, who happens to be the brother-in-law of his cousin's best friend, then your cab will be allowed to make a U-turn on Shanghai's Nanjing Lu during rush hour while traffic is halted on both sides until it is safely on its way.

As is the case with other great philosophical concepts, there is much that is both positive and negative in Confucianism. After China became a republic in 1911 Chinese leaders continued to place Confucius on a pedestal and promote his teachings. The cult of Confucius is still very much alive today: not only in mainland China and Taiwan, but also in Japan, Korea, Malaysia, Singapore, Vietnam and South-East Asia, as well as in Chinatowns in major cities throughout the world.

The birthday of 'China's First Educator' – 28 September – is still celebrated as Teacher's Day in Communist China. Confucian ideals are said to have laid the spiritual cornerstone for the successful union of authoritarian government and American capitalism in the five 'Asian Tiger' nations of Japan, Korea, Taiwan, Hong Kong and Singapore. In October 1994 the Communist regime held an enormous symposium in Beijing to celebrate Confucius' 2545th birthday. The keynote speaker was Lee Kuan-yew, former Prime Minister and *éminence grise* of Singapore, who was invited because he had merged Confucian thinking with western technology in bringing prosperity and harmony to his city-state.

During my grandfather's youth in imperial China a son or daughter who used abusive language to his parents or grand-parents could be punished by being put to death. Conversely, if a son violated the law and committed a serious crime against the emperor, his parents and grandparents could be punished with him under the assumption that they had failed in their duty to educate him properly.

Grandfather's parents had total control over the lives of their children. They were the ones who chose their children's spouse, education, career and everything else. Filial piety was enforced rigorously by Chinese law. When there was a dispute between parent and child, the law was always on the side of the parent. Should a parent murder his child, the authorities would not intervene. This was the foundation of Confucian 'justice'.

Things were very different when we moved to Hong Kong in 1949. Like King Lear, my grandfather had become financially dependent on my parents and my stepmother was a cruel woman. He never complained but once he told me, 'One of the most pleasing features of life in Shanghai in the old days was the respect shown by the youth at large towards anyone with grey hairs, even if he should be a poor, blind and homeless beggar.'

My Ye Ye died long ago, but on my trips to Hong Kong or Shanghai I always think of his remark when I see well-dressed Chinese professionals solicitously escorting their toothless or semi-paralysed elderly parents to restaurants and other public places. From the nods of approval I observe on the faces of passers-by, I know the public still view these filial acts as the epitome of virtue. As I watch the son (or daughter) attend to his feeble and petulant parent with the same care and obedience he was taught in childhood, I can't help wishing that my grandfather could come back and see it too.

Should the west adopt some laws and some Asian values to protect the rights and happiness of the elderly? In America and England the young are often ashamed to be seen in the company of their grandparents. Instead of being treated with honour and obedience, the old are cast aside and neglected. Far from being proud of their experience and wisdom, many seem ashamed of their advanced years. Everything else being equal, wouldn't it be better to grow old in a Confucian world than in a western world? Without respect, love and affection from their children, what is there for the elderly to look forward to?

It has been said that every Chinese wears a Confucian thinking cap. My daughter, Ann, visited us when I was doing the research for this chapter. One evening, while watching television, we saw an old clip of President Nixon telling the nation, during the Watergate Scandal, that he was not a crook. I remember saying to Ann, 'A president leads by his moral power. If he cannot set an example by his moral behaviour, he will lose the loyalty and trust of all those who elected him.' Later, while reading the *Analects*, I noticed with a shock of recognition that these thoughts came straight from Confucius.

5

Look Inwards for Salvation

回頭是岸

HUI TOU SHI AN

During the two years I spent working and studying in Edinburgh I took a course in medical hypnosis as part of my post-graduate training. After a few introductory lectures our professor instructed us to hypnotise each other to gain 'hands on' experience.

My 'partner', Dr Gupta, was a strapping young man from Bombay who happened to be sitting next to me. To my amazement, after I had followed a few simple directions on a printed form on how to induce hypnosis, Dr Gupta immediately fell into a deep trance. At first I thought he was teasing me by pretending to be under my control. It was simply too easy. My unexpected success also terrified me. I was afraid I would never be able to wake him again. However, that proved to be trouble-free as well.

Then came my turn to be hypnotised. But no matter how hard Dr Gupta tried and how willingly I cooperated, it simply wouldn't work. After two hours we finally gave up. Dr Gupta was very disappointed. So was I. It just didn't seem fair that while he allowed himself to be hypnotised by me, I could not reciprocate in kind.

When I started my research on Hinduism, Buddhism and Zen Buddhism, this episode came back to me. Neither Dr Gupta nor I realised it then, but the outcome of our attempts at mutual hypnotic induction was predictable. It is apparently much easier to bring about a hypnotic trance in someone with a cultural heritage from eastern India than in someone from China. Perhaps we Chinese are simply too distrustful or too practical to let go of our psyche. In a way, this difference also symbolises the underlying divergence between Hinduism, Buddhism and Zen Buddhism.

The roots of Buddhism came from India around 500 BC, when a splinter group broke away in revolt against Hinduism. In the middle of the second century Buddhism spread to China, where it merged with Taoism and Confucianism to become syncretised into a special brand of Chinese Buddhism called Zen Buddhism.

The spiritual source of Hinduism can be traced to a body of ancient 'revealed scriptures' called the Vedas, which were brought to India 4000 years ago by fair-skinned Aryan nomads from Russia and Persia.

Hindus believe that every living thing is the same in essence, and that divinity exists in all animate and inanimate matter. Hence every creature is considered worthy of veneration. However, behind this complex polytheism lies a single fundamental principle known as Brahman, the supreme essence of life. Human beings can, through personal effort and the attainment of inner knowledge, reach union with Brahman while still on earth because this ultimate reality and the individual soul are actually one and the same: 'That art thou.'

Hindus do not believe that they have an exclusive hold on religious truth. They concede some validity to all religions and tend to assimilate rather than exclude: Buddha is merely another incarnation of one of their more popular gods, Vishnu, as are Muhammad and Jesus. They view the world as a relative reality and teach a 'live and let live' tolerance.

Hindus believe in *karma* and reincarnation. *Karma* is a system of penalties or rewards for bad or good deeds performed in former lives. Since human fate is largely predestined, the Hindi view is one of acceptance. Reincarnation is inextricably tied to *karma*. Each person has existed before (as a human being, beast or insect) and will exist again and again until he finally escapes by attaining union with Brahman the Divine.

Practices such as meditation, prayer and yoga are considered essential in joining or yoking the individual soul to Brahman. Yoga aims to discipline the unconscious by controlling the breath as well as involuntary bodily processes such as heart-beat in order to release the soul from earthly bonds. A guru, spiritual instructor or enlightened being often attracts a group of like-minded pupils who seek guidance (from the guru) for their spiritual development. Together, they lead a life of simplicity and meditation in a secluded community known as an *ashram*.

There are four major castes in Hinduism. The highest are the Brahmins or spiritual leaders. Next come the nobles and warriors, then the merchants and artisans. The fourth caste consists of the menial workers. Below these four are the 'untouchables'. The original function of this system was to teach surrender, acceptance and happiness within one's given situation. However, as with any organised structure, there is a potential for distortion and this has led to discriminatory practices. Buddhism emerged as a revolt against Hinduism but adopted many Hindi beliefs.

Buddha lived from 563 to 483 BC. His family name was Siddhartha Gautama and he was the son of a ruler of a small state in northern India, on the border with Nepal. He was married and had a son, and led a sheltered life of luxury behind his palace gates. One day he ventured out to survey his kingdom and was distressed to observe for the first time the suffering, sickness and poverty all around. At the age of twenty-nine, unable to reconcile himself to the inequity of a world where he had so much while others had so little, he gave up his privileged life to become a religious wanderer, practising meditation and asceticism in an attempt to abolish pain and suffering.

At that time there were many other wandering gurus in India in revolt against Hinduism, which had developed into a highly ritualistic and discriminatory religious organisation controlled entirely by the Brahmins, who were considered the sole interpreters of the Vedas and therefore the arbiters of morality. Gautama began by rejecting the authority of the Vedas, all the Vedic gods and the entire caste system.

Legend tells us that Gautama attained enlightenment while meditating under a fig tree. From then on, he was known as the Buddha, the Awakened or Enlightened One. He organised his followers into a regulated community, declared that anyone (even women) could be admitted to the formal fellowship of Buddhist disciples (Sangha), removed all caste discrimination, and expounded moral principles.

The oldest existing complete collection of Buddhist scriptures (written in the Indian language of Pali) was introduced into Sri Lanka (Ceylon) by Buddhist missionaries in the third century BC. Known as the Pali canon (also the Theravada or Hinayana canon), it purports to be written in the language used by Buddha himself.

Like Hindus, Buddhists believe that the life we live now is not the only life, but one of a great series of lives that extends far back into the past and stretches into future lives unless we attain enlightenment. The balance of the account of good and bad deeds (our accumulated *karma*) in our present life determines our fate in our next life. *Nirvana* means the absorption of one's soul into the supreme soul of the universe and permanent release from the ceaseless round of rebirths. In Buddhist teaching, *karma* provides an opportunity as well as a way of escape into *nirvana*.

Buddhists believe that we all have the potential to become enlightened in this lifetime but that we must find our own path. In this search, Buddha emphasised that extremes of self-indulgence or self-mortification should both be avoided. He advised following a middle road. Enlightenment consists of recognition of the Four Basic Noble Truths:

- that pain and suffering are common in life;
- that human cravings often give rise to unhappiness;
- that by relinquishing cravings and desires, much suffering can be avoided;
- and that pain can be avoided by following the noble eightfold path of behaviour: right view, right thought, right speech, right action, right livelihood, right effort, right mindfulness and right concentration.

In short, that the unceasing human desire for ego satisfaction keeps the wheel of cause and effect in ceaseless motion. This wheel exemplifies the eternal karmic round of existence.

Buddha expressed himself in these words: 'I, Buddha, who wept with all my brothers' tears, whose heart was broken by a whole world's woe, laugh and am glad, for there is liberty! Ho! Ye who suffer! Know ye suffer from yourself.'*

Approximately one hundred years after Gautama's death, a schism occurred and his community divided into two schools during the Second Great Buddhist Council held at Vesali. The Conservative School of the Elders continued to adhere strictly to the original Pali doctrine by withdrawing from the world. This came to be known as the Theravada or Hinayana (small vehicle) and is the form of Buddhism practised today in Sri Lanka, Burma, Thailand, Laos and Cambodia.

The second school, known as the Mahayana (large vehicle), spread to China, Japan, Korea, Nepal and Tibet. Mahayana Buddhism holds a much more liberal, tolerant and pliant view on the interpretation of the Pali canon. Over the centuries Hinayana Buddhism declined in India under the pressures of Vedic ritualism and Hinduism, while Mahayana Buddhism took hold and flourished abroad. Mahayana teachings encourage adherents to become involved in secular life and allow far greater freedom in the development of new ideas to conform with local customs and beliefs. Consequently, Tibetan Buddhism became markedly different from Zen Buddhism, although both belong to the Mahayana school. Over the centuries, Zen Buddhism took on a uniquely Chinese flavour and diverged more and more from other types of Buddhism.

The Japanese character zen 禅 is actually the same word as the Chinese character chan 禅, although it is pronounced differently. The Japanese adopted many Chinese characters

* G. Parulski, *A Path to Oriental Wisdom*, 1976, page 50.

78

in the development of their language. These adopted characters are called *kanji* in Japanese. *Kanji* in Chinese is pronounced *han* 漢 *zi* 字. The two characters mean 'Chinese words' in both languages. The character *zen* or *chan* was originally derived from the Indian word *dhyana*, which means 'meditation'.

Zen Buddhism claims to transmit the essence of Buddha by allowing the individual to experience the enlightenment which Buddha attained. Zen is entirely different from Indian meditation. The noted Chinese scholar Dr Hu Shih once described Zen as a 'reformation or revolution in Buddhism'. Perhaps Zen's revolt arose because many Chinese simply found it impossible to achieve a state of transcendentalism no matter how hard they practised yoga. Finally, Chinese Buddhist masters encouraged their disciples to find *nirvana* while going about their daily business. Students were taught according to their individual needs, characters, circumstances and personalities. The aim of Zen is to awaken the student to the realisation of his own enlightenment, not only through traditional meditation but also through stories, questions, *koans* (see page 89) and the rituals, customs, expressions and activities of daily life.

Zen has no creed and does not involve committing oneself to certain definite rules of behaviour. It is concerned not with faith but with wisdom, knowledge and experience. Unlike Christianity, which has a creed and a code spelt out in the Ten Commandments, Zen suggests certain principles of action that help people to discover for themselves the meaning lying at the root of Buddhism.

The Chinese are considered to be a practical, sceptical and 'this-worldly' people. When asked about the afterlife, Confucius answered in six words, '*Bu zhi sheng, yan zhi si?*' (Not know life, how know death?) His teaching was rational, earthy and people-oriented. And yet, it seemed that Confucianism alone was not quite enough. Despite their pragmatic and worldly exterior, the people were actually starved of answers to questions regarding their inner life. As Buddhism took hold and spread throughout China, Chinese thinking underwent a profound change. People wondered about the meaning of life and began to ask themselves, 'In the beginning, was there being, or not being?' and, 'Where does the road [of life] begin and where does it end?'

One day, when my son Roger was five years old, we were driving along the freeway on our way to a basketball game, a distance of forty miles. He sat there watching the cars whizzing by, completely mesmerised by the seemingly endless ride. Suddenly, he turned to me and asked, 'Where does the freeway begin and where does it end?'

The earliest evidence of Buddhism in China is to be found in the year 2 BC, when it was recorded that a foreign diplomat had given instruction on Buddhist teachings to a Chinese minister. Chinese translations of Buddhist scriptures, however, did not appear until the middle of the second century AD. These first renderings were taken from the Pali canon, but from the fifth century on, most of the Buddhist scripts were from Mahayana Buddhism.

During the fourth and early fifth centuries two Buddhist monks, Kumarajiva (344–413) and his pupil Seng Chao 僧肇 (383–414), translated ninety-four separate Buddhist philosophical texts into Chinese with succinct lucidity and logic. The Sanskrit word for 'path' (*marga*) was translated as *tao*.

The word *tao* has had mystical connotations from ancient times and was described by Lao Zi thus:

Something undefined and yet complete
Was born before heaven and earth
Silent and boundless
Existing alone and forever unchanged
Pervading over all without fail
She may be considered 'Mother of all under heaven'
I know not her name
I call her the Tao
And in the absence of knowledge
I name her the Great.

This ancient Chinese concept of the *tao* now merged with Buddhist mysticism to give Chinese Buddhism a breadth and profundity undreamt of in the original Sanskrit texts. The word *buddha* in Sanskrit means 'aware'. 'Buddha-mind' was therefore interpreted as a state of consciousness of the *tao* attained through meditation (*zen*). Besides meaning the 'path to enlightenment', the Chinese Buddhist *tao* also began to imply that Buddhism was the 'path to truth' as well as the 'ultimate meaning of life'. The Buddhist spirit of 'emptiness' was integrated with Lao Zi's mysterious 'oneness', and teacher and pupil were instrumental in developing a systematic Chinese Buddhist philosophy for the first time.

Half Indian and half Kuchen, Kumarajiva was a child prodigy, became a monk at the age of seven and enjoyed a reputation as a brilliant scholar in India. His fame travelled far and wide and in AD 384 a king of the Former Chin dynasty dispatched a general to bring him to China. He stayed with the general for seventeen years; then, in 401, another king of the Later Chin dynasty sent an army to escort him to the capital city of Chang An. There he was accorded the highest honours and the title of National Teacher. He was encouraged to organise a bureau and his daily lectures were attended by audiences of over a thousand monks.

His pupil, Seng Chao, was born into a poor family. Forced to make his living by repairing and copying books, he educated himself and read voraciously. Although he enjoyed the works of Lao Zi and Zhuang Zi, he was bowled over by Kumarajiva's translations of the Buddhist scriptures. After his conversion to Buddhism he became a monk. In AD 398, when he was only fifteen years old, he travelled west in search of Kumarajiva and later followed him to Chang An. Besides helping Kumarajiva with his translations, he wrote on his own. His ideas gradually bridged the gap between Taoism and Buddhism and he incorporated many Taoist and Confucian concepts into a new Chinese Buddhist philosophy. Seng Chao's idealised Buddhist state became strikingly similar to Zhuang Zi's vision of becoming one with the universe and harmonising with all things (see page 40).

Seng Chao argued that the concepts of motion and rest imply *time.* But time is unreal because the present cannot be either in the past or not in the past. If it is in the past, it is of course not in the present, and if it is not in the past, what is there to cause its present existence? Since there is no past in the present and no present in the past, time is unreal. The same argument stands for the past and the future.

Having concluded that time was impossible, Seng Chao argued that motion was also an illusion because motion depends on time: the only thing which is permanent and continues for countless generations is *merit.* According to the Buddhist doctrine of *karma,* good deeds bring merit, which influences the future favourably.

Seng Chao was only thirty-one years old when he died in AD 414, barely one year after the demise of his mentor Kumarajiva.

When I was eleven years old, my parents enrolled me as a boarder at the Sacred Heart Canossian Convent School in Hong Kong. Lessons were conducted in English but our teachers were Italian nuns. Religion was a required course of study and we read the Bible every day. I believed everything the nuns taught me and yearned to be baptised a Catholic like my fellow pupils.

We were encouraged to go home every third weekend and Sundays were 'visiting days' but no one ever came for me. Finally, one freezing Chinese New Year when I was twelve, my parents did send a car and I was allowed to go home for the first time. In those days they lived in a rented three-bedroom flat on Boundary Street in Kowloon. They told me to sleep on a cot in my grandfather's room and I was happy. I knew he and I would have a chance to talk. Besides, I was simply dying to tell him all about my religion, and perhaps even convert him.

That first night home, after dinner, I sat hunched on the floor in Ye Ye's room with a blanket wrapped around my shoulders. Outside I could hear the sound of wind and rain beating angrily against the windowpane. Even today, after so many years have passed, I remember the smell of his cigar, the glow of the electric heater, the expression of concern in his eyes, the comfort of being understood, and the conviction that he cared.

During our talk I repeatedly questioned his Buddhist beliefs with the brash confidence of adolescence. Full of my new-found faith, I tried to preach Catholicism to him with the help of my Bible and the English–Chinese dictionary.

It was an uphill battle. To my dismay, I discovered that many English terms simply did not exist in Chinese. I was unable to explain certain key concepts because I lacked the proper Chinese words to express them. When I looked up the English expressions in the dictionary, the Chinese translations did not represent what I was trying to depict.

Ye Ye had particular trouble with the words 'Jesus', 'miracle' and 'sin'. 'You say Jesus is God as well as the son of God,' he commented. 'How can He be both? And then you can't even tell me His surname! In China in the old days emperors were called "Sons of Heaven" but every emperor had a surname!

'As for miracles, that's all very well. But you tell me a miracle is supposed to transcend the *tao* [i.e. the laws of nature]. That's an impossibility, I'm afraid. The *tao*, by its very definition, can never be transcended. The *tao* that can be transcended is not the true *tao*.

'Then there is sin. You say sin is a crime (罪 *zui*) of the heart. If sin means "crime", then the sinners, like criminals, should be punished by flogging or imprisonment.'

We went round and round. Finally I repeated Sister Louisa's words: 'In the end, you have to have faith.'

'Faith!' he exclaimed. 'But you haven't convinced me yet! You are asking me to accept blindly a whole system of dogmas contained in your foreign book. Why should I? If you give me logical proof and evidence, I would not need faith. I only need faith when I substitute my wish to please you for the evidence that you have been unable to provide.'

'What about your Buddhism then? Why should your feelings be different there? How does it differ from Christianity?'

'Buddhism never claimed to be the only existing truth. In fact, it welcomes other religions and considers them to be different paths leading to the *tao*. It involves no creeds. One is not asked to commit oneself to certain definite rituals and commandments from Gautama Buddha. In fact, for many years no Buddha images were made. Instead, Buddha was represented

84

by a footprint, an empty throne, or a robe and alms bowl.

'Buddhism is not about faith. It is about self-awakening. The potentiality for awareness is within each of us. *Hui tou shi an* (look inwards for salvation). However, there are barriers that need to be removed before we can reach our inner wisdom and uncover our Buddha-nature. The best way is by meditation. The aim of meditation is to train our mind towards intuitive wisdom. When meditating, try to think of nothing and let your mind go free. Focus on your breathing. Keep a smile on your face. With practice, you can meditate while sitting, walking, working or going about your daily business. Activities such as calligraphy, drawing, playing music, flower arrangement and gardening are particularly conducive to self-awareness.'

'Without the Ten Commandments, how will you know what is good and what is evil?' I persisted.

'We Buddhists believe that if we are enlightened, then our lives will be expressions of our ethics. If we should behave unethically, then we are not enlightened. There *is* no perfect ideal outside of ourselves and our behaviour at any given moment.'

'If Buddhism came from India, why is it more popular in China and Japan than in India?'

'This is an excellent question. Part of the reason may have been due to language. The two Buddhist monks Kumarajiva and Seng Chao skilfully translated Buddhist teaching into Taoist terms to make it easier for Chinese people to understand. I believe Zen's success may have been due to its progressive integration with the philosophy culled from ancient Chinese classics.'

'The nuns at school encourage us to go to church every morning. On Sundays they take us to the cathedral for high mass. It's so peaceful to kneel in front of the altar and listen to organ music. Is there anything similar in your Buddhist temple?'

'No. There are no scheduled Sunday services at the temple. However, both in Tianjin and Shanghai a group of us used to meet at seven o'clock every morning in the local park and practise *tai chi* and *qi gong* [see page 42]. We would then sit in a circle and meditate while my friend Lao Wu played music on his *erhu*. Some Sundays I'd bring you with me and once Lao Wu even let you play his instrument – do you remember?'

'Yes, I remember. Lots of times you'd all just sit there on the grass with your legs crossed and eyes closed saying nothing.'

'We were concentrating on drawing our mind inward and focusing on our breathing. Conscious breathing unites body and mind and makes us whole. Gradually, we learned to nourish awareness in each moment and bring mindfulness to every action. From then on, we could meditate while standing, walking or even doing chores.'

'At other times you'd say "Amitabha" over and over. Why?'

'There is a sect called the Pure Land Buddhists who believe in a buddha named Amitabha who lives in a wonderful western paradise. All those who concentrated on reciting the holy name Amitabha would end up there and achieve salvation. At first I found that hard to believe. However, by repeatedly uttering "Amitabha", I did discover something wonderful. I was filling myself with positive *qi* [energy]. I take a deep breath, chant "Amitabha" ten times, then make a conscious effort to smile. Amazingly, by carrying out this simple ritual a few times, my mind seems to become clearer and calmer. Now I do it frequently, especially when I'm upset. Just the other day the thought suddenly struck me that the Pure Land Buddhists were correct after all.'

'But you don't go to the park any more.'

A look of weariness came over him and he said sadly, 'Things are different here in Hong Kong. I don't know the way and I can't speak the dialect. So I try to meditate and practise *tai chi* on the balcony. But it's not the same. I miss the trees, bushes, plants, flowers and rocks. Most of all, I miss my friends . . .' He saw the tears welling up in my eyes and added quickly, 'One day, if you live long enough to be as old as your grandfather, you'll understand what I'm telling you tonight. Who knows, your children may even ask you the same questions. Fifty years from now, don't be surprised if you find yourself quoting from the *Tao Te Ching*. Meanwhile, you have to begin your own journey and find your own answers.'

At the end of the New Year holidays I went back to school. A few months later I was baptised a Catholic. Although the nuns sent formal written invitations to my parents, no one came to attend the ceremony. On the day of my baptism I was the only convert not accompanied by anyone from home.

After the death of Kumarajiva and Seng Chao their disciples – as well as the six Buddhist patriarchs who came later – continued to take the best of Indian Buddhism to further the development of Chinese Buddhism. Each contributed in his way to integrate Buddhist teaching with different philosophies from the Chinese classics. Of the six, Bodhidharma (AD 460–534) came to China from India in AD 520 and is venerated as the first Zen Buddhist patriarch. He taught that all awareness was connected with Buddha-nature; and that 'Nature, Mind, Buddha, Path and Zen' were inexorably linked. Hui Neng 惠能, the sixth and last patriarch, founded the School of Sudden Enlightenment and emphasised that

87

anyone, from peasant to emperor, could attain that state.

Hui Neng was born in Canton and orphaned at the age of three. Poor and illiterate, he made his living by peddling firewood. One day, while stacking timber in his shack, he overheard a preacher expounding the teachings of Buddha on the street outside. Fascinated, he questioned the sermoniser and discovered that he had just come from a Buddhist monastery up north, where about a thousand monks were studying under the direction of the fifth patriarch, Hung Ren 弘忍. Setting out at once, he found Hung Ren and told him that he was searching for the Law of Buddha. After interviewing him, Hung Ren put him to work in the rice-pounding room.

One day eight months later, the fifth patriarch suddenly summoned all his pupils and announced that he wished to select his successor. Each disciple was to write a verse and the one who understood best the Law of the Buddha was to become the sixth patriarch and be given Buddha's old robe.

At midnight Shen Xiu 神秀 (AD 605–706), the head monk, held up a candle and wrote the following verse on a wall outside the fifth patriarch's hall:

The body is like a tree so wise
The mind is like a mirror bright
Hour by hour we clean and wipe
Lest dust should fall and dim the light.

The master was not completely satisfied. He told Shen Xiu that he was at the front door of understanding Buddhism but had not yet entered and should try again.

Meanwhile, Hui Neng had also composed a poem, which he dictated to a friend to transcribe:

Neither is there a tree that's wise
Nor is there a mirror bright

Since Buddha-nature is clear and pure,
Whereon can dust alight?

On reading this, the master realised at once that Hui Neng had understood his teaching and attained Buddha-nature because he no longer harboured any doubts. He waited till midnight, called Hui Neng to his hall, gave him the robe which had originally belonged to Buddha himself and appointed him to be his successor.

The incident described above, along with Hui Neng's collection of sermons, was transcribed by one of his disciples in the book *Liu Zu Tan Jing* 六祖壇經 (*Platform Scriptures of the Sixth Patriarch*). This ancient document from the Tang dynasty was discovered at the Tun Huang caves in north-west China by the Hungarian-British archaeologist Sir Arthur Stein in 1901 and presented to the British Library in London.

Legend tells us that enlightenment was sometimes achieved through certain experiences known as *koans* in Japanese and *gong an* 公案 in Chinese: *gong* means 'public'; *an* means 'case'. Literally, a *koan* is a legal term referring to a case where the decision given has set a precedent for subsequent cases. Zen masters borrowed the term to describe a situation which creates a temporary impasse because it cannot be solved within the usual frame of reference. In seeking a solution, the student has to alter and redefine his frame of reference, thereby deepening his insight and comprehension of the truth. Quite often the *koan* consists merely of a question and an enigmatic answer:

A pupil seeks out a Zen master in order to be enlightened. The master invites him to have a cup of tea. The tea arrives and the master courteously hands the pupil a cup of tea. He then starts pouring more tea into the cup. The cup is full but the master continues to pour although tea is spilling over from the cup onto the table and floor.

'Master!' cries the pupil. 'The cup is full.'

'Exactly,' answers the master. 'How can I instruct you unless you have first emptied your mind?'

Among serious Buddhist scholars, Zen is understood to be concerned mainly with self-awareness. It aims to transform man's consciousness about himself and the universe.

When I was thirteen years old, I developed pneumonia. After my discharge from hospital, my stepmother allowed me to go home for a few days to recuperate before returning to boarding school. One afternoon while she was out, Grandfather took me to a Chinese teashop for tea and *dim sum*.

It was an old-fashioned establishment with square, red-wood tables and quaint round stools, whirring overhead fans and latticed windows. Like prisoners granted a few hours' reprieve, the two of us stuffed ourselves with dumplings, noodles, pots of fragrant jasmine tea and a delicious, milky soya bean soup blended with grated Chinese broccoli.

Towards the end of the meal, as I raised the last spoonful of steaming soup to my lips, I gave a scream of horror. Lying at the bottom of the large soup bowl was the distinct, brown shape of a dead cockroach. As of that moment, the thought of having drunk the soup became unbearable. Pointing to the insect, I turned to Ye Ye. To my amazement, he went on calmly drinking his soup, spoonful by spoonful.

'I feel sick to my stomach!' I cried, adding irritably, 'How can you go on drinking that soup?! Can't you see the cockroach? You're going to be poisoned!'

'How can I miss seeing the cockroach when you are raising such a ruckus?' he replied. 'But this soup is piping hot and that insect looks as if it's been stewed for a while. You yourself were just saying how tasty the soup is. Nothing has changed. Why shouldn't I go on enjoying it?'

'But everything has changed!' I told him. 'You didn't know there was a cockroach in the soup before. Now you know! So how can you continue drinking?'

My grandfather put his spoon down beside his empty bowl and said patiently, 'Before you saw the cockroach, you loved the soup. As soon as you became aware of the insect, you loathed the soup instead. Yet the soup has not changed. It is only your perception of it that has altered. Knowledge of the cockroach's presence transformed your attitude radically.

'The older I get, the more I appreciate the importance of attitude on our understanding and enjoyment of life. From time to time, bad things happen to all of us. We can't change that. However, we certainly can control our attitude in dealing with life's misfortunes.

'You see a dead cockroach and suddenly you think you've been poisoned; even though the soup was delicious and the cockroach has obviously been boiled to death. How do you know it wasn't a special ingredient added by the chef to enhance the soup's flavour?

'You are always challenging me about my Buddhist beliefs and asking for proof. But proof is all around us. Look at the perfection of these flowers on our table! As our great philosopher Wang Pi* wrote, "Nature never errs. Things always follow their principles. Though complex, they are never chaotic. Though

* (AD 226–249)

91

many, they are not confused." When you perceive the wondrous orderliness of nature, you know very well it could not have happened randomly.

'To return to your soup, the truth was that it was hot and delicious. The presence of the cockroach should not detract from this fact. Just as the absence of miracles should not prejudice you against Buddhism. In fact, this very absence supports my Buddhist beliefs. A miracle can only happen when Nature's laws are transcended. According to Buddhism, this is an impossibility because the *tao* is true and eternal.

'Remember: for you to become enlightened, the transformation has to come from within you yourself.'

In our modern world's headlong rush towards speed, profit, efficiency and progress, we tend to lose sight of the details of our true nature. These days, more and more westerners are looking for answers from eastern thought in their search for their inner being. They seem lost and feel a need to find their way.

Westerners often speak of 'the battle of life' or 'conquering nature', as if we humans were engaged in a hostile takeover bid against the universe. When the Wright brothers built and successfully flew their plane, the newspapers reported that they had 'won the *fight* against gravity'. The Zen view is that human beings cannot be separated from their environment. We are one and the same. The Wright brothers' plane did not abolish gravity but merely learned to adapt to the *li* (principle) of gravity. Every living organism is part of the universe and the universe is made up of all of us. When we pollute our environment to suit our convenience we are destroying part of ourselves because we and the universe are one and the same. Ecological awareness may be perceived as part of the Zen experience.

The concept of God is somewhat different in the east from that in the west. In America and Europe God is perceived as the creator of the universe who is in control of everything and everyone. In order to change our fate, we need to pray to Him and He may or may not respond. The Zen view is that the *tao* is the cause of all being; the universe exists in an orderly form according to three principles originally derived from the concepts of Taoism and Confucianism: *li* 理, *zi ran* 自然 and *wu wei* 無為.

Li means 'principle' or 'order of nature'. Since the *tao* is the cause of all being, therefore the *tao* puts things in order. *Li* is manifested in the beauty we perceive all around us (in a grain of sand, a snowflake, a wild flower, a waterfall or a rock). The uniqueness of this 'principle' is difficult to put into words but we recognise it as soon as we see it. *Li* is also manifested in the logic of mathematics, the symmetry of nucleotides in a strand of DNA, the wisdom of a Solomon who looks beyond the law to administer true justice, or the markings in the grain of wood. When a quarrel arises in China, both sides are urged to *jiang li* 講理 (speak the *li*) or plead the case according to 'principle'.

During my studies and long years of medical practice I was continually amazed by the *li* demonstrated by the human body, ranging from the development of the embryo from a single fertilised ovum to the mysterious capacity of brain cells for intelligent thought. As Karl once exclaimed when explaining the biophysics of the human eye, 'Oh! The complexity of it! Oh! The humanity of it!'

Zi ran has been translated as 'Nature'. It also means 'sponta-neity' or 'doing that which comes naturally'. *Zi* means 'one-self'; *ran* means 'correct'. The Zen interpretation of *zi ran* is 'to act according to the *li* inherent in the *tao*': 'Let everything do that which is of itself.'

As I explained earlier, *wu wei* means 'taking no unnatural action' or 'arriving at action through non-action' (see page 34). As a first-year medical student, I was taught first and fore-most 'to do no harm' because with proper support and nourish-ment, the human body has an enormous capacity to heal itself. The syncretic Zen view is that the universe is perfect in itself and should not be 'coerced' or 'forced' to conform to human desires. This is the true meaning of *wu wei*.

My twenty-four-year-old daughter Ann came home last Christ-mas from New York, where she works as an editorial assistant at a large publishing firm. We spoke of her latest project – a book written by a prominent Buddhist monk. Though she had attended a Catholic high school we seldom discussed religion. To my surprise, she asked me about Buddhism. The conver-sation brought me back to that chilly Chinese New Year in Hong Kong and I found myself thinking of my grandfather as I told her:

'Gautama Buddha never claimed to be a prophet and Buddh-ism is not a religion in the western sense of the word. Instead, Zen Buddhism is about living and the acquirement of self-awareness through living. The development of Zen Buddhism is closely linked to the philosophy of Lao Zi and Zhuang Zi. To get a clearer picture, you might like to get a book called the *Tao Te Ching* out of the library and read the last four lines of Chapter 25.

Man acts according to the order of the earth,
Earth acts according to the order of Heaven,
Heaven acts according to the order of the Tao,
The Tao does that which comes naturally (*zi ran*).

'Some writers consider the *Tao Te Ching* to be the greatest book ever written. Among them was the British poet Philip Larkin. When I was your age I was doubtful but that was a long time ago. Nowadays, I tend to agree.'

6

Thousands and Tens of Thousands of Varieties of Qi

氣象萬千

QI XIANG WAN QIAN

When I was a little girl I lived in Tianjin, in north-east China. The summers there were dry, hot and sunny. On the few occasions when the skies were overcast, my Aunt Baba would take us children into the garden in the evening twilight to enjoy the cool breezes (*chun feng liang*). I remember watching the clouds hovering in parallel, horizontal white layers against patches of bright blue sky. I believe these thin strips of greyish-white clouds may have been the pictorial origin of the word *qi*, which initially meant 'air, vapour or gas'.

The strokes in *qi* may have evolved in the following way:

二　≡　气

Later, the character for rice (米 *mi*) became incorporated into the ancient form of the word *qi* 氣. This may have come about from observing the 'nourishing' steam rising out of a saucepan of boiling rice. Thus, the concept of *qi* came to encompass and symbolise nourishment as well as vapour.

Qi (pronounced *chee*) is a difficult word to translate and probably no two scholars will agree on its exact definition. It is a unique concept fundamental to Chinese thought, and has no equivalent in English. In the west a 'rational' and 'scientific' way of perceiving reality is to divide it into

| Matter | vs | Spirit |
| Form | vs | Space |

Matter and form are viewed as solid and concrete phenomena that can be seen and felt. Spirit and space are more ephemeral concepts. It is difficult to accept a word conveying something that encompasses matter, spirit, form and space all at the same time, but such a word is *qi*.

In the Chinese–English dictionary *qi* occupies more than half a page. Translated literally, the word means 'air, gas, breath or life-force'. Then there are physical types of *qi*, such as *kung qi* 空氣 (atmospheric air), *tian qi* 天氣 (*qi* of the sky or weather) and *du qi* 毒氣 (poison gas); as well as abstract *qi* expressing human emotions, such as *guan qi* 官氣 (*qi* of a bureaucrat throwing his 'weight' around) and *pi qi* 脾氣 (*qi* of the spleen or temper). Every artist attempts to capture the incomparable vital force of nature called *yuan qi* 元氣 and incorporate its essence into his work. When a painter succeeds we tell him 'he has arrived' and is exhibiting *qi xiang wan qian* 氣象萬千 (thousand and tens of thousand varieties of *qi*). Sometimes, however, when this occurs and he is appointed to paint the portrait of the governor, he may start to cultivate notions of his own importance and show signs of *qi ling xiao han* 氣凌霄漢 (spewing overbearing *qi* all the way to the sky). It is possible that when the governor sees the work he will be unimpressed and refuse to pay. This gets our artist upset and *sheng qi* 生氣 (his *qi* is generated and stirred up). He bursts out with anger (*qi shi ziong ziong* 氣勢兇兇); so much so that his hair bristles with rage against his hat (*nu fa chong guan* 怒髮衝冠)! Altogether a very bad hair day!

Qi can be divided into two primary types. The innate *qi* or *yuan qi* of a person is the basic *qi* he has inherited from his parents. (The concept of *yuan qi* is so ingrained among the Japanese that instead of saying, 'How are you?' or, 'How is your health?' a standard greeting in Japan is, 'How is your *yuan qi?*')

Acquired *qi* is the *qi* a person gets from air, food and social interaction. It can be replenished by a healthy diet, physical exercise, undisturbed sleep, good friends and laughter.

The Early Han dynasty writer and philosopher Dong Zhong Shu 董仲舒 (179–104 BC) defined *qi* this way:

> Within the universe exists this *qi* of *yin* and *yang* in which man is constantly immersed, just as fish are immersed in water. The only difference between *qi* and water is that water is visible whereas *qi* is not. But man's existence is as much dependent on this *qi* as fish's life is dependent on water. *Qi* is found everywhere in the universe but is less visible than water. Thus although the universe seems to be empty, yet there is substance at the same time. Man is engulfed in this vortex and, regardless of whether he is orderly or disorderly, is carried along on and on, in a common current.

The Song dynasty philosopher Zhu Xi 朱熹 (1130–1200) had this to say: 'At first there was form (形 *xing*) and matter (質 *zhi*). *Qi* then infused form and matter. *Qi* is the primordial energy which is the source of all beginnings.'

The concept of *qi* is integral to Chinese thoughts on medicine and philosophy. The theory of Chinese medicine is based on traditional Chinese beliefs of *yin/yang*, *qi* and the five elements (see page 21). In the *Yellow Emperor's Classic of Internal Medicine* (黃帝內經 *Huang Di Nei Jing*), from the second century BC, *qi* plays a prominent role. The ancient Chinese thought that *qi* had its own circulatory system separate from that of the blood, although the two systems were intimately intertwined. They believed that the movement of *qi* (breath or air) influenced the flow of blood. What, then, directs *qi*? It is directed by *yi* 意 (intention of the mind). Thus, *qi* was seen as a psycho-physiological force connected to the flow of breath, blood and inner thoughts.

One of the most tragic cases I ever witnessed as a physician was that of a fifty-two-year-old widow, who was admitted to hospital with acute abdominal pain. Exploration under anaesthesia revealed a massive inoperable tumour causing a blockage of the major arteries supplying her intestines. The surgeon in charge had no alternative but to close her wound and inform her of the terrible diagnosis.

The patient was devastated. She asked how long she had to live and was told less than two weeks. She expressed a desire to be kept alive long enough to have one last conversation with her only son Daniel, who was mountain-climbing in Nepal.

Despite everyone's best efforts, Daniel could not be located. Six weeks went by. Our patient lapsed into a coma but did not die. Finally, on a Monday morning forty-five days after her surgery, Daniel rushed into the intensive care unit. He knelt by her bedside, called her 'Mom' and kissed her hand. To everyone's amazement, she opened her eyes and smiled at him.

Later that day she died. There was no doubt in anyone's mind that she had been waiting for a last glimpse of Daniel before departing (or, as we Chinese would say, 'giving up her *qi*'). I remember telling Daniel that his mother's *qi*, directed by the intention of her mind, was what had sustained her long after her surgeon's predicted date for her death.

Although there is no anatomical evidence for the existence of a separate circulatory system for *qi*, it is generally acknowledged that we humans do possess an intimate 'mind–body' connection. Studies have shown that depression, anxiety and stress may cause or aggravate numerous systemic diseases (such as hypertension, angina, arrhythmia, rheumatoid arthritis and asthma), whereas tranquillity, laughter and happiness can alleviate pain, promote health and improve immunity.

According to *Huang Di Nei Jing*, all illnesses are due to insufficiently balanced *qi*. It asks, 'If the true *qi* is harmonious, how can illness arise? . . . True *qi* will come if you remain calm and imperturbable. Develop your inner spirit and you will have well-being.'

When *qi* is weak, exhausted or inadequate (a condition described as *xu* 虛), its flow becomes disharmonious and the patient is susceptible to disease. When angry, *qi* is aroused. When happy, *qi* is strengthened (*gu* 固) and flows smoothly. When sad or anxious, *qi* is diminished. When frightened, *qi* is confused. Chinese medicine aims to transform *qi* (*qi hua* 氣化) through a healthy diet, physical exercise and peace of mind. If *qi* is in harmony (*qi he* 氣和), immunity is replenished. The *Classic* also states:

> The function of the tract-channel system of the human body is to promote a normal passage of blood and *qi*

101

so that the vital essentials derived from man's food can nourish the *yin* and *yang* viscera, sustain the muscles, sinews and bones, and lubricate the joints ... What we call the vascular system is like dykes and retaining walls forming a circle of tunnels which control the path that is traversed by blood so that it cannot escape or find anywhere to leak away.

The Chinese believe that the balance of *yin* and *yang* within the body is the fundamental condition of harmony. When *qi* is obstructed, its flow is impeded and an imbalance of *yin* and *yang* is created. Through proper diet, herbs and acupuncture, the flow of *qi* is restored, thus re-establishing harmony through the balance of *yin/yang* energy.

When I was ten and living in Shanghai, my Aunt Baba noticed a lump in her breast. As my parents were away in Tianjin, she asked me to accompany her when she consulted a traditional Chinese doctor. After waiting for over an hour in a packed waiting room, we were admitted into the inner office. The doctor was an old man dressed in a Chinese robe with white hair and a flowing white beard. Patiently, he wrote down my aunt's complaints. Then he took her left hand, placed four fingers on her wrist and sat in deep concentration with his eyes closed for ten minutes without saying a word.

My aunt was looking at me with a resigned and anxious expression. I tried to come to her rescue. 'Doctor,' I began timidly, 'my aunt has a lump in her body. There is nothing wrong with her wrist.'

'I am well aware of that!' he replied. 'When you are older, you will come to realise that everything in one's body depends on the flow of *qi*. That flow is carried by blood and reflected in the twenty-eight types of pulses which I can differentiate. By her pulse, I can detect any type of illness she may be suffering from. In a way, you can say that her pulse is tapping out her diagnosis and transmitting it to me through my fingers.'

After that, he wrote a prescription while expounding on the circulation of *qi* and meridians, *yin* and *yang*, solid organs called *zang* 臟, hollow organs named *fu* 腑, and the five elements. Neither Aunt Baba nor I fully understood what he was talking about, nor could we read the complicated characters he scribbled with brush and ink. Nevertheless, we listened respectfully and took the prescriptions with us into an adjacent room, where we paid our bill. After this, a clerk stood in front of a strange-looking wooden cabinet with about 100 little drawers, each neatly labelled. Prescription in hand, he went from drawer to drawer and carefully weighed out an assortment of herbs into different paper envelopes. He gave the whole lot to Aunt Baba with instructions on how each was to be brewed and when it should be taken. We left the doctor's office without him examining any part of Aunt Baba but her wrist.

My aunt took the medicine as instructed. Not long afterwards, my stepmother separated us. We met again thirty-one years later. I asked Aunt Baba about her breast mass. She told me it had never gone away but had remained the same all those years.

Just about everyone in China, from the poorest peasant to the greatest scholar, believes in the power of *qi*. In *The Art of War* 兵法 (*Bing Fa*), a remarkable book written by Sun Zi 孫子 2500 years ago, *qi* is much emphasised. At one time this treatise on war and strategy was reserved for rulers and not permitted in private hands. If the book was discovered in the secret possession of an ordinary individual it was construed as evidence of a military conspiracy; thus its contents had to be transmitted orally. Eventually, when censorship became less stringent, it was transcribed onto bamboo slips or pieces of silk and stored in imperial libraries. A few copies have been discovered buried in caskets next to the bodies of ancient kings together with their precious jewels and cherished swords.

For over 2000 years *The Art of War* has remained the most important military treatise in China, assiduously studied by all her military leaders. Its fame spread to Japan and Korea and it became a sort of ageless international bestseller on warfare. Translated by a French missionary 200 years ago, it was reputedly read by Napoleon, Bismarck, Nazi generals and the Japanese army, as well as by West Point cadets in the USA. Chiang Kai-shek and Mao Zedong were both familiar with its text and based their military strategies on its teachings. According to the British historian Basil Liddell Hart, 'Sun Zi's essays on war have never been surpassed in comprehensiveness and depth of understanding. They might well be termed the concentrated essence of wisdom on the conduct of war.'

'If a country is to wage a successful war,' wrote Sun Zi, 'then the people in that state must be well governed by a compassionate and dynamic ruler who enjoys support and loyalty from his people and his officials. The soldiers will then march into battle filled with morale, momentum, determination and intensity. This is known as military *qi*.'

In the opinion of Sun Zi, *qi* ebbed and flowed constantly. He advised that the enemy should be attacked when their *qi* had abated:

The *qi* of the enemy can be snatched away, the commanding general's mind can be seized. For this reason in the morning their *qi* is ardent; during the day their *qi* becomes indolent; at dusk their *qi* is exhausted. Thus one who excels at employing the army avoids their ardent *qi*, and strikes when it is indolent or exhausted. This is the way to manipulate *qi*.

In Chinese philosophy, *qi* is the counterpart of *li*. *Li* means principle, reason or logic (see page 93). *Qi* means both energy and matter. It is considered to be the fundamental substance, the powerful life-force that exists within each and every one of us.

The Song dynasty scholar Zhang Zai 張載 (1020–77) wrote, 'If *qi* integrates, its visibility becomes potent and physical form appears. If *qi* does not integrate, its visibility is inadequate and there is no physical form. Therefore, in some cases *qi* becomes form and in others it remains space.'

In many ways, the ancient Chinese concept of the relativity of 'matter' and 'space' is surprisingly modern. According to Einstein's theory of relativity, the only thing constant about our universe is that nothing is constant. Though Einstein's equations clearly showed that the universe was either expanding or shrinking in time but never staying the same, he himself was reluctant to accept this. The notion of an ever-changing universe was so unpalatable that he initially refuted his own logic and modified his calculations by introducing a 'cosmological constant' in order to explain away his own computation. Twelve years later the American astronomer Edwin Hubble established by measurements of distant galaxies that the universe is indeed expanding. Realising that he had blundered, Einstein admitted his error and returned to his original conclusions. Since then, numerous scientists have confirmed Hubble's observations and Einstein's theories but, to me, it is truly astonishing that the ancient Chinese manual *I Ching* had already proclaimed over 3000 years ago that everything in the world is ruled by an immutable law of change, thus predating Hubble and Einstein by more than thirty centuries.

Qi also has parallels in modern physics. The behaviour of elementary particles in the study of quantum mechanics have been described by Fritjof Capra this way:

> The high-energy scattering experiments of the past decades have shown us the dynamic and ever-changing nature of the particle world in the most striking way. Matter has appeared in these experiments as completely mutable. All particles can be transmuted into other particles; they can be created from energy and can vanish into energy. In this world, classical concepts like 'elementary particle', 'material substance' or 'isolated object' have lost their meaning; the whole universe appears as a dynamic web of inseparable energy patterns.
>
> The distinction between matter and empty space finally had to be abandoned when it became evident that virtual particles can come into being spontaneously out of the void, and vanish again into the void . . . the vacuum is far from empty. On the contrary, it contains an unlimited number of particles which come into being and vanish without end.

Thus matter and energy are part of a single continuum known as the 'quantum field'. The ancient Chinese concept of *qi*, then, may be the modern equivalent of this quantum field, which is constantly creating and disintegrating matter at the same time.

The Chinese philosopher Zhuang Zi wrote, 'Human life

arises from the coming together of *qi*; if it comes together there is life, and if it goes asunder, there is death.' To the Chinese mind, *qi* is the powerful and mysterious life-force that exists within all things. Humans are a part of the whole *qi* prevailing in Heaven and on earth. The earth's magnetic field is merely one aspect of this enigmatic energy.

When I lived in Shanghai, dinner was a solemn affair. As soon as the bell sounded at 7.25 p.m., my siblings and I would file down the stairs to the dining room with our hair combed and hands washed. Passing my father's room on the first floor, I often saw him crouched beside his short-wave radio, listening intently with his ear glued to the instrument.

Once I questioned my grandfather: 'What is Dia Dia listening to, Ye Ye?'

'News broadcasts in English from the BBC in London, England. He listens to the twelve-o'clock news.'

'Twelve-o'clock news! But it's after seven o'clock in the evening!'

'That's Shanghai time. Over there in London, it's noon time.'

'How far is London?'

'Thousands of miles from Shanghai. Halfway around the world in Europe.'

'Are they broadcasting from London now?'

'Of course! This very minute.'

'How can their voices travel so far, so fast?'

'This is due to the magical *qi* of the English. When you grow up, you must learn from them.'

Years later, after the death of my grandfather, I was lucky enough to win a writing competition that indirectly enabled me to go to school in London. There I learned about electro-magnetic waves, light waves, radio waves, sound waves and many other kinds of waves. I was told that our understanding of nature had been transformed by the theory of relativity and quantum mechanics. Recently, I read in Brian Greene's *The Elegant Universe* that the 'super-string' theory may be the uni-fied field theory that eluded Einstein for the last thirty years of his life. Through it all, I could not help asking myself at each new revelation, over and over, Is this what the ancient Chinese philosophers meant by the word *qi*?

I shall now relate to you a personal story involving my own *qi*:

My stepmother Niang* died of cancer of the colon in 1990. Exactly one day before the reading of her will I discovered that I had unexpectedly and mysteriously been disinherited. In addition, I later found out that there had been a conspiracy on the part of my siblings to hide the truth from me before her death.

Two of my attorney friends approached me and advised me to challenge my Niang's will. They said they would charge me nothing because they were convinced I would be given a portion of my parents' estate if I allowed them to file a caveat on my behalf.

At first I was sorely tempted because I was simply outraged by my family's deception. There is nothing worse than the knowledge that you have been deliberately duped and robbed

---

* *Niang* 娘 is a Chinese word that means 'mother'.

by those you trust, who you believed would guide and protect you. I was depressed, angry and desperately unhappy. I suffered from insomnia and loss of appetite. Again and again I tried to talk to my brother James, who was the executor of our parents' estate. However, he was in denial and had no wish to speak to me.

Full of resentment, I flew to Shanghai and unburdened myself to my Aunt Baba, whom I loved very much. I spoke to her of lawyers and jurisdiction, of my agony at being victimised and my quest for justice. This is what she said to me:

'If you take your siblings to court, I predict that you will become more unhappy; because even if you were to win after a long, legal battle, it would be a hollow and negative victory since money is not the issue nor your motivation. Besides, no court on earth can ever compensate you sufficiently for your emotional pain.

'Let me remind you of our ancient Chinese concept of *qi*. What is *qi*? It stands for the vital energy that permeates the universe, regulating and balancing each person's vitality. Used correctly, the word *qi* means the foundation of courage, will and intention.

'*Qi* is dependent on moral conviction. If you feel in your heart that you are right, you will go forth even against thousands and tens of thousands. But if you feel in your heart that you are wrong, you must stand in fear even though your opponent is the least formidable of foes. Right now, your whole being is infused with your *qi*. Go and do something positive with it. Life is similar to a game of chess. Think clearly before you act. By giving up this pawn, you might conceivably end up winning the entire contest. Always bear in mind what our great scholar Sun Zi wrote in his book *The Art of War*. Being unconquerable lies with yourself; being conquerable lies with the enemy. One who knows the enemy and knows herself will not be endangered in a hundred engagements. But the best way is to win without fighting.'

So, instead of suing, I started writing long letters to my brother James, to which there was never a reply. Then a strange and exciting thing started happening. The more I wrote about the problems of our family being torn apart and in conflict with itself, the calmer I became as I went about my daily tasks. Gradually, as the months went by, my insomnia vanished. My appetite returned. My outlook improved. I started playing tennis again and sleeping more soundly. Even my bowel habits became regular. At the end of two years I realised that I had the first draft of a publishable manuscript in my hands. So I gave up my job as a physician and started looking for an agent. Call it bibliotherapy. Call it serendipity. But that's how I became a writer. In a way, you could say that my book *Falling Leaves* is a visual manifestation of the integration of my *qi*.

7

Let Food be Medicine

以食為療

YI SHI WEI LIAO

'One fundamental difference between us Chinese and the English is this,' I once told my brother James when I was visiting him in his medieval rooms at Cambridge. 'We Chinese live to eat, whereas the English eat to live.'

'There is another even more significant variance,' he replied. 'To the English, the most important component for happiness is sex. To us Chinese, it is food.'

'Do you remember,' I reminisced nostalgically, 'the treats we used to get at the different festivals? Moon cakes stuffed with bean paste at the Autumn Moon festival. Sautéed sticky rice cakes at Chinese New Years. My favourite, however, were the *zhong zi* 粽子 we used to eat on the day of the Dragon Boat festival . . .'

'You mean Wu Yue Jie 五月節 [Fifth Month festival or 'Double Fifth']! It's only called Dragon Boat festival by the British! You should call it by its proper name. After all,' he

111

added with a touch of asperity, 'even if you're going to medical school in London, you're still Chinese, not British!'

I decided to ignore his remark and continued, 'Double Fifth! I thought the festival occurred some time in June! Why did we eat *zhong zi* on that day, anyway?'

James explained that he was talking about the Chinese lunar calendar based on the moon going around the earth, not the western Gregorian calendar based on the earth going around the sun. The fifth day of the fifth lunar month usually lands on the day of the summer solstice in June. This festival is based on the tragic life of Qu Yuan 屈原, a virtuous minister of the state of Chu during the fourth century BC, who committed suicide in Tung Ting lake to draw attention to the corruption at the court of the king. His body was never recovered and the villagers used to throw food into the lake for his sustenance. Apparently, Qu Yuan's spirit appeared to the villagers and complained that their offerings were being intercepted by a monster. To prevent this from happening again, he gave instructions for the food to be wrapped in bamboo leaves and prepared according to a special recipe. The packets were to be tied with five differently coloured silk threads. Inside were cakes made of glutinous rice, roast pork, chestnuts, lotus seed, green bean and the yolk of salted eggs. 'That's the *zhong zi* you've been dreaming about,' James concluded.

'The Italian nuns at my school in Hong Kong took us boarders to Aberdeen one summer to see a dragon boat race. I remember all the colourful boats, the drummers beating out the strokes, the waving banners and the noisy fire crackers. The lead boat's hull was painted emerald green; its "face" was covered with a bright red beard and its tail was made of blue feathers like a peacock. Afterwards we had a picnic and the sisters bought *zhong zi* from a street hawker. They were piping hot and difficult to unwrap. Mother Valentino finally had to cut the threads with a pair of nail clippers. When I opened mine, a delicious bamboo fragrance hit my nostrils. I bit into the glistening sweet rice, which was filled with ground dates and ginkgo nuts. It was the best thing I had ever tasted.'

'The type you had was called "long life sweet *zhong zi*",' James told me. 'It's supposed to improve your memory as well as your health. Strange how Chinese food is always associated with notions of health. You can hardly speak of one without mentioning the other. Here in England, nobody would dream of telling you, "This is good for your health" when they hand you your plate of fish and chips or bacon and eggs. But in China, food and medicine appear to be the same thing. That's all we ever think about.'

Indeed, we Chinese are obsessed with food. Our standard greeting on meeting a friend is not, 'How are you?' but, 'Have you eaten your meal (*fan** 飯) today?' At an all-Chinese gathering the conversation usually centres around a dish, a dinner or a restaurant. We anticipate, discuss, comment, praise, criticise, condemn, dream, plan, debate and exchange information on the subject constantly. Mention the name of a café serving superb Shanghai crab to any Chinese who grew up in the old country and you'll see him brighten at once. We travel long distances and pay high prices for a good meal.

The knowledge and enjoyment of cuisine is considered an

---

* The word *fan* means 'meal' as well as 'cooked rice'. Rice is the staple in southern China. Uncooked rice is called *mi* .

art as well as a measure of culture. Renowned statesmen and intellectuals did not think it beneath them to eulogise a dish in their writings. It was not considered demeaning for famous poets and philosophers to rhapsodise over food in song and verse. Thus we have a pork dish (*Dong Po* 東坡肉 pork) named after a Song dynasty poet and a chicken dish (*Zuo Gong* 左公雞 chicken) called after a famous general.

Most Chinese are gourmets and would agree with the French gastronome Brillat-Savarin that 'the discovery of a new dish does more for the happiness of mankind than the discovery of a new star'. The French are well known to be serious about their cuisine, but few people realise how earnest we Chinese are about our food as well. The difference is that, as far as cooking is concerned, the French have done the most with the most while the Chinese have done the most with the least.

Because of over-population and frequent natural disasters, famine was common in China.

Once, when my parents were away in Tianjin, my aunt and I sneaked some hot soup out of the kitchen and poured it into the tin bowl of a little girl begging at our door. Even today, I can remember her scrawny, hunched shoulders and the elation in her eyes as she held the steaming vessel to her lips with both hands and eagerly slurped its contents.

People were often hungry, and practically everything edible became an item for consumption. Foods we consider delicious range from dried seafood (such as shrimps, scallops, sea cucumbers, oysters, jellyfish, shark's fins and seaweed); to 'bird's nest'; and dried fruits and vegetables such as tangerine peel, melon seeds, lily flowers, mushrooms, cloud ear* (*yun er* 雲耳) and bean thread. In the west many of these would have been tossed into garbage cans without a second glance.

The exotic-sounding 'bird's nest', for instance, is actually a protein regurgitated by swallows and harvested from their nests built high on the cliffs and ravines overlooking the ocean. Creamy yellow in colour, it comes in curled, thin, dry strips and has a glossy, hard surface. Like bean curd, it has a subtle flavour and blends well with other ingredients cooked with it. Unlike bean curd, it requires hours of soaking, cleaning and removal of feathers. Perhaps because of this, it is prohibitively expensive and has become a status symbol and a 'must' for formal banquets in China. However, many would agree that it tastes rather insipid.

In the province of Sichuan there is a delicious duck dish flavoured with a special spice called *dong chong xia cao* 冬蟲夏草 . Once, a Chinese microbiologist colleague of my husband's sitting next to me at dinner in Cheng Dou, capital of Sichuan, told me that this spice was, in reality, a mummified caterpillar that was parasitised and killed by a fungus: hence its worm-like appearance. As I was mulling over this piece of information which, I must admit, immediately diminished my erstwhile enthusiasm for the dish, he added that it was also a great tonic and very *bu* (nourishing and beneficial). 'This spice is unique because it combines *yin* and *yang*. As its name implies, its life

---

* Cloud ears are similar to wood ears (*mu er* 易). Both are bracket fungi with a delicate flavour. They defend against heart attacks by prolonging the bleeding time and preventing blood clots from forming in coronary vessels.

is divided into two phases. It starts off as a caterpillar in winter and then turns into a vegetable in summer. *Dong chong xia cao* means "winter worm, summer grass". Traditional Chinese doctors,' he went on loftily, 'prescribe *dong chong xia cao* for consumption, joint pains and aching in the loin. Nowadays, we are discovering some interesting beneficial properties from fungi isolated from this animal/vegetable, spice/herb. They appear to strengthen our immune system.'

'During my childhood in Shanghai,' I replied, 'I used to see children eating bark peeled off the sycamore trees lining the street on which we lived. Perhaps one day this, too, will be used in Chinese cooking.'

Rice is the basis of every meal in the south, whereas steamed bread, noodles and millet are the staples in the north. *Cai* 菜, the word for vegetables, also means a 'dish to go with rice'. Meat is generally sliced into thin slivers and cooked with the vegetables, almost like a condiment.

This unique way of cooking may have developed because of food scarcity and poverty but, ironically, the traditional Chinese peasants' diet is now viewed by many western physicians as the 'ideal' diet to maintain health, prevent obesity and prolong life. Because meat, oil and fuel were expensive and in short supply, the frugal Chinese farmer fed his family almost exclusively on grain (rice) and vegetables. Meat, usually pork, was eaten only on major feast days such as Chinese New Year. For ordinary Chinese people, a satisfying meal consists of steamed rice, soup and two different *cai* to accompany the rice: there is frequently a plate of fresh vegetables stir-fried with small slices of meat or fish and/or a bean curd dish.

The wok was probably invented in order to conserve fuel

and oil. This thin, round-bottomed metal cooking pan allows a minute quantity of oil to be spread evenly and extensively, then heated very rapidly. Its large cooking area provides a perfect surface for stir-frying, braising, steaming, stewing or poaching. Many professional chefs consider the wok to be the most ingenious cooking utensil ever devised.

In preparing Chinese food, meat and vegetables are traditionally cut up into small bite-sized pieces before cooking, in order to blend flavours and save fuel. This practice is so long-standing that during the Zhou dynasty (1027–256 BC), cooking used to be called *ge* 割 *peng* 烹. *Ge* means 'to cut' and *peng* means 'to boil or cook'.

My father used to take frequent trips to Europe and America with my Eurasian stepmother, Niang. She would complain that no matter which city they visited, he insisted on dining at Chinese restaurants. Once, they were invited to lunch at a renowned French establishment in Paris that had been awarded three stars by *Guide Michelin*. While there, my father hardly touched his veal chops, spinach purée and cheese soufflé. As soon as the party broke up, however, he entered a nearby Cantonese café. There, he wolfed down two bowls of boiled rice, fried bean curd with mushrooms and sautéed cabbage with ham. When Niang protested, he stood his ground.

'Without rice, my stomach is uncomfortable and I feel as if I haven't eaten properly,' he told her.

'Couldn't you at least have waited until you were back at the hotel and then gone out again? Mister Baker and Monsieur Trudeau probably spotted you rushing into this place immediately after saying goodbye. They were still waiting for their taxi!' (Baker was father's English banker and Trudeau his financial analyst. During lunch, Trudeau had attacked his lobster with gusto whereas Baker had picked at his roast beef with a preoccupied air, seemingly far too important to bother with anything as frivolous as food.)

Father brushed her objections aside. 'The problem with western food is that it is boring. Everything is cooked separately. It's so unimaginative to see a hunk of meat all on its own without any vegetables to blend in the flavours. Served that way, the meat looks lonely and unappetising. Then there are never any vegetables to speak of. Instead of stir-frying my spinach with a little garlic, they boiled it to death and threw away the best part, the water in which it was boiled. It would have made such a refreshing clear broth! On top of that, there was no rice!'

'How can you eat rice day in and day out without getting tired of it?' Niang interjected. 'Doesn't your palate need a change?'

'Do you get tired of drinking water when you are thirsty?' Father asked rhetorically. 'Of course not! Rice is just as fundamental. Remember the wine-tasting we went to yesterday? We were each given a glass of water and told to rinse our mouths between sips of wine so that we could appreciate the different flavours more fully. The same theory goes for rice. It is our Chinese equivalent. I eat a piece of bean curd. Then a little rice. Have a mushroom or two. Neutralise it with rice. Take in a mouthful of cabbage. Another chopstickful of rice. And so on. Otherwise all the tastes get jumbled up!'

This was an on-going sore point between them. Like many Chinese, Father was inclined toward vegetarianism. His favourite meal consisted of steamed rice, bean curd, fresh vegetables in season, and salted fish.

Taoism and Buddhism may have played a major role in creating the almost meat-free diet preferred by my father. Taoism emphasised a return to nature; whereas Buddhism had an injunction against killing. Both schools of thought encouraged abstention from meat. Even today, many Chinese lean toward vegetarianism, though few are strict vegetarians. There is a Chinese saying that 'Meat eaters are contemptible'.

Although my stepmother was actually half French and half Chinese, she considered herself French. She hated green vegetables and liked meat, especially beef. After Father came down with Alzheimer's disease, Niang no longer had to please him. For ten years she ate the same lunch every day: a piece of char-grilled *filet mignon* cooked medium rare served on its own. Perhaps as a result of her diet, she developed cancer of the colon and died at the age of sixty-nine.*

Immediately after the funeral of my grandmother at the Buddhist Temple in Tianjin in 1943, our relatives and friends followed us home. A lengthy and elaborate vegetarian meal was then served. Although our food was normally prepared by a male chef and seven maids, this particular 'banquet' had been catered from the temple. Dishes of *cai* were stored in stacked bamboo steamers and delivered by Buddhist monks with shaven heads. Course followed course, including mock squab, mock duck,

---

* It is now known that charcoal-grilled fatty animal meat (e.g. beef steaks cooked at high heat) contains potent carcinogens (such as polycyclic aromatic hydrocarbons and amines) that may cause cancer of the colon in susceptible individuals. Eating cruciferous vegetables like cauliflower and broccoli may prevent cancers from occurring.

mock ham and mock spicy chicken. All the 'meats' were made of wheat gluten or bean-curd sheets but looked and tasted exactly like their namesakes. For dessert we had chewy sweet sesame dumplings, glazed apples and eight treasure pudding (*ba bao fan* 八寶飯). The pudding consisted of jujubes (Chinese dates), apricots, lychee nuts, pears, peaches, lotus seeds and red bean paste cooked in glutinous rice. Everyone laughed when my eldest brother proclaimed it the best meal in his entire life. Then he added, 'Can I please have the same meal again next month? Then I wouldn't feel so guilty enjoying it.'

Throughout China's long history famine and natural disasters were ever-present possibilities. Life expectancy has been short and malnutrition common. Food was scarce and was perceived as nourishing and healing. Gradually, the Chinese came to believe that, depending on the condition, many foods were curative. Whatever is good for the body is considered food as well as medicine. Sun Se-miao 孫思邈, a Chinese herbalist living in the sixth century AD, wrote, 'A good doctor first discovers the cause of a disease. Having found it, he tries to cure it initially by food. He only prescribes medicine when food is ineffective.' The expression 'You are what you eat' is equivalent to the Chinese saying of '*Yi shi wei liao*' (Let food be medicine).

Approximately one quarter of the drugs used in the western world today are made from plants. In China a regime known as *shi liao* 食療 (diet therapy) is being pursued at various medical establishments, which are developing specific recipes aimed at fighting diseases such as diabetes, high blood pressure, atherosclerosis and cancer. Instead of taking prescription drugs and undergoing surgery, each patient is encouraged to follow a specific diet tailor-made to treat his particular condition, prescribed by physicians who are also experts in nutrition.

In the second half of the twentieth century Nathan Pritikin came to agree with this ancient Chinese concept of the health-giving properties of food. Suspecting that cholesterol in the diet was one of the major causes of cardiovascular disease, he developed the low-fat, low-cholesterol Pritikin diet. The importance of diet in promoting health and preventing disease is now widely recognised and accepted.

The Longs were heirs to one of the greatest fortunes in America. One day Dr Tony Temple, a physician friend, visited his patient John Long at his home in Florida, where John was recovering from a recent heart attack. Tests done while John was in hospital had revealed that he also suffered from high cholesterol as well as prostate cancer.

On entering the house, Tony noticed six shabbily dressed Chinese workmen laying butterfly tiles in the backyard. John's wife explained that she was building a Chinese garden and had hired this crew from Suzhou, in the People's Republic of China. Though uneducated, the men were experienced and skilful at laying tiles.

John was sitting up in bed eating lunch. Tony was horrified to see cream of mushroom soup, lamb chops with French fries and apple pie à la mode on his tray. 'This meal is full of fat and cholesterol. It's bad for your heart and prostate. You need fresh vegetables and bean curd. Why don't you try the Pritikin diet?' he admonished.

'It's so tasteless! I tried it but I can't eat that stuff. I want to enjoy my food! Eating should be a pleasure, not a duty.'

At that moment they became aware of the most delicious aroma of sizzling onions and garlic emanating from the garden. Tony opened the shutters and peered out. Sitting on their haunches around a portable stove, the Chinese workmen were lunching on fresh tomato soup, steamed rice, stir-fried cabbage and a wokful of spicy bean curd sautéed with garlic and chillies. With a shock, Tony and the Longs suddenly realised that six penniless labourers from China were eating healthier and better-tasting food than their billionaire American employer!

The word for 'physician' in Chinese is *yi sheng* 醫生 (healer of life), denoting a holistic herbal approach as contrasted to the western view of the physician as a curer of disease. Traditional Chinese 'medicines' consist not of injections, pills or elixirs, but of plant and/or animal ingredients brewed into a tea, a soup or a stew. Emphasis is given to its appearance and flavour. Foods considered particularly restorative are described as *bu*. These are supposed to replenish and strengthen a patient's *qi* (see page 98), thereby improving his immunity and increasing his chances of self-healing.

In the west foods are divided either biochemically (into proteins, fats and carbohydrates), or calorically (into fattening or non-fattening). The Cantonese in southern China tend to divide foods into two major categories: hot or cool.

Hot *re* 熱 foods produce *re qi* 熱氣 (hot *qi*), which can be beneficial or harmful, depending on the patient's condition at any one time. Good *re qi* generates energy, improves the digestion and stimulates the metabolism. Bad *re qi* exacerbates infections and fevers. Ginger, chilli peppers, garlic, chestnuts and beef are some examples of *re* foods.

Cool *liang* 涼 foods generate *liang qi* 涼氣 (cold *qi*). Again, the same food can be good or bad at different times. Good *liang qi* is cleansing and soothing. It relieves fevers and other manifestations of excessive *re qi*, such as blisters and ulcers, and aids digestion. Excessive *liang qi* causes a runny nose, diarrhoea and malaise. Cucumbers, watercress, lettuce and most fruits are considered *liang* foods.

The concept of 'hot' or 'cool' foods corresponds with the Chinese idea of separating the universe into *yin/yang* opposites that merge into one another in a continuous cycle (see page 18). Health is regarded as a condition of balance between the body and mind as well as the body and the environment. Illness happens when this balance is disturbed. The aim of a physician is to restore this balance or, better still, to keep the patient in such good health that disease can be avoided altogether.

In traditional Chinese medicine foods are used as tonics to ward off or 'mend' the effects of harmful environmental factors (such as smoke, dust, cold, heat or germs) and combat stress, loss, depression and fatigue. Prescribing medicine to cure a disease (rather than preventing the disease through eating a proper diet) is considered to be too little too late: somewhat like 'trying to march in after the enemy has already occupied the city'.

As a child walking to and from school along the Avenue Joffre in Shanghai, I often used to stop at a particularly grand Chinese medicine shop to peer through the windows. It was difficult to tell the difference between this 'herbal pharmacy' and a large grocery store. Clearly labelled jars of leaves, roots, bark, stems, fungi and ginseng stood side by side with rhinoceros horns, deer antlers, pieces of bones, dried mushrooms, birds' nests, wood ears, sharks' fins, jujube (Chinese dates), dried tangerine peel, dragons' eyes (a delicious round fruit) and bottles of Chinese wine. Some of these bottles even contained exotic ingredients such as tigers' tendons floating in a dark liquid.

On one occasion when I came down with a cough, runny nose and high fever, Aunt Baba went down to the kitchen herself and brewed me a large bowl of delicious soup, served piping hot and thick with a mysterious assortment of ingredients, including various herbs, dates, ginkgo nuts, ham, chicken, winter-melon and mushrooms. The best part was that she allowed me to lie there propped up on three pillows while she fed me as if I were still a baby. Even today, I remember the worry lines on her forehead as she blew on the soup, spoonful by spoonful, to cool it before placing it in my mouth. 'The doctor who saw you yesterday told me that your *qi* is not in harmony,' she told me. 'You are a very lucky girl because your doctor practises traditional Chinese medicine and not western medicine. So he prescribed this delicious soup for you instead of painful injections and nasty pills. It will accomplish the same purpose: induce perspiration, banish fever and balance your *qi* so that you will get well again.'

For some reason I started to cry. Why? I hardly knew myself. Was it because my head hurt and my joints ached? Or was it because I had no words to express this feeling of hollowness inside. I wanted to tell her how grateful I was to see her sitting by my side. I knew very well that although the house was full of people, I was of no significance and counted for nothing. In fact, she and my Ye Ye were probably the only two people in the entire world to whom I mattered. Nobody else cared whether I was sick or depressed, lonely or afraid, hungry or cold, alive or dead.

She dried my tears and teased me. 'Now! Now! Nine years old and still crying like a baby! What am I going to do with you! If you give me a big smile, I'll bring you a surprise! That's better! I might as well tell you. For dessert, you're going to get a whole pear stuffed with herbs and stewed for a long time in a small clay pot.'

Even though I was hot with fever, at that moment I felt happy and safe. My parents weren't due back from Tianjin until the following week and my aunt was in charge while they were away. I asked her for the recipe of the medicinal soup and pear and she wrote them down for me. That night I dreamt I was very ill and was admitted to the local hospital, which turned out to be a fancy restaurant! The patients were all served their meals (by waiters in tuxedos) while lying in bed. When the doctor came to do his rounds, he carried in his hands not a book of medicine but a cookbook with a menu attached. He felt my pulse and told me that my *yin* and *yang* were out of synchrony, copied a 'prescription' from his cookbook and handed it to me. It turned out to be a recipe for my favourite hot-and-sour soup! Unfortunately I woke up before I had a chance to taste my new medicine.

Soya beans have been grown in China since before the age of written history. Introduced into Britain and cultivated in the Royal Botanic Gardens at Kew in 1790, the soya bean plant was said to have been brought from Europe to the USA by Thomas Jefferson. Fresh soya beans (known as *edamame* in Japanese) are delicious when boiled and served cold. The shelled green beans have a nutty flavour but the fuzzy pods are inedible. The Chinese stir-fry fresh soya beans with mushrooms, bamboo shoots or other vegetables and serve them with rice.

Soya beans can be processed into bean curd (tofu, which can also be freeze-dried), soya milk, soya milk powder, soya protein concentrates, textured vegetable protein (TVP), soya flour and soya oil. Fermented soya beans can be made into soya sauce, Chinese bean paste or Japanese miso.

The four soya bean products which are used most extensively in China are: bean curd, soya sauce, bean paste and bean curd sheets. Soya sauce and bean paste are both manufactured by fermenting the soya bean. This process was already in use during the Zhou dynasty (1100–255 BC): ancient writings of that period record that an imperial cook was appointed to provide 120 jars of fermented soya bean per year for imperial use. According to *Shih Ji* 史記 (*Record of History*), written during the Early Han dynasty (206 BC–AD 23), many merchants acquired wealth and titles through the manufacture and sale of soya bean products.

Tofu (bean curd) was first made by Liu An 劉安 (died 122 BC) during the Han dynasty. The word *to* 豆 (pronounced *dough*), means 'bean'; the word *fu* 腐 means 'fermented'. Tofu means fermented bean or bean curd. To make tofu, dried soya beans are softened by soaking them in water. Then they are ground together with water into a milk-like liquid. This 'milk' is then coagulated with gypsum (calcium sulphate) into tofu. Long considered indispensable in Chinese cooking, high in proteins, vitamins and fibre and low in cost, bean curd has the unique ability of absorbing and enhancing the flavours of meat, fish, herbs or any other food cooked with it.

Historically, soya foods were believed by the Chinese to possess beneficial properties. For breakfast every morning, my grandfather used to drink a bowl of hot soya milk to 'ward off the cold and nourish his *qi*'.

Nowadays, western scientists are becoming increasingly aware that soya beans do contain various unique substances called phytochemicals and oligosaccharides, which help to prevent certain diseases. Phytochemicals are biochemicals produced by plants that are known to promote health. Among those discovered in the soya bean are the isoflavones Genistein and Daidzein which, together with soya proteins, appear to prevent breast cancer in women and prostate cancer in men. In addition, isoflavones lower cholesterol and prevent heart disease; preserve bone density and hinder osteoporosis in post-menopausal women; reduce hot flushes during menopause; and improve kidney function.

Oligosaccharides are sugars that have recently been discovered to play an important health role. They stimulate the growth of 'good' intestinal bacteria such as bifidobacteria. The bonds of these sugars are not digested by any of the enzymes in the small intestine, thereby allowing them to reach the large intestine (colon) intact.

How do soya beans prevent cancer? Depending on the site and type of cancer, isoflavones and oligosaccharides play separate and different roles. The isoflavones have a similar structure to the naturally occurring human hormone called oestrogen. Breast cancer is caused when oestrogens combine with oestrogen receptors in breast cells. Isoflavones 'compete' with human oestrogens by binding with the same receptors and blocking the entry of the oestrogens. In this way they help to prevent the onset of breast cancer. In addition, they appear to hinder the formation of new blood vessels at cancerous tumour sites as well as slow down the activity of 'cancer enzymes' that convert normal cells to cancer cells. Hence, soya reduces the likelihood of developing many other types of cancer besides breast cancer, for example prostate cancer.

The oligosaccharides play their beneficial role mainly within the large intestine. They appear to enhance the growth of 'beneficial' bacteria while inhibiting the growth of 'harmful' bacteria, thereby helping to prevent the development of colon cancer and ulcerative colitis.

How do soya beans lower cholesterol and prevent heart disease? Since soya bean is a vegetable and contains no cholesterol, eating soya products (instead of meat) and drinking soya milk (instead of cow's milk) will naturally lower blood cholesterol. Studies have further shown that soya lowers the levels of 'bad' or low-density lipo-proteins in the blood, while levels of 'good' or high-density lipo-proteins remain the same. Soya also prevents cholesterol from harming the body by inhibiting its oxidation. Lastly, soya seems to reduce blood-clotting and plaque-formation in blood vessels, thus preventing heart attacks, strokes and angina.

How do soya beans prevent osteoporosis? Eating lots of animal protein appears to leach calcium from our bones and cause it to be excreted. Calcium loss leads to osteoporosis. Soya actually inhibits the breakdown of bones, thus preserving bone density. The previously mentioned oligosaccharides in soya also seem to facilitate calcium absorption from the large intestine. In addition, tofu is made using calcium sulphate (gypsum), which makes it calcium rich. Fortified soya milk, soya beans and textured vegetable protein are all good sources of calcium.

How do soya beans help during the menopause? Menopausal symptoms such as night sweats, hot flushes, insomnia, anxiety and irritability are due to the reduced production of oestrogen. It is interesting to note that in China there is no equivalent term for menopause or hot flushes. The English–Chinese dictionary published by the Oxford University Press in 1994 uses twelve Chinese characters to translate menopause as 'time for females aged around 50 when monthly periods cease'. Since the isoflavones in soya are known to exert a weak oestrogenic effect, perhaps a lifelong diet of tofu and soya beans has provided Chinese women with sufficient isoflavones to lessen their menopausal symptoms.

How do soya beans help to prevent kidney disease? The kidneys consist of millions of tiny filters that separate unwanted chemicals from the blood and excrete them into the urine. In people with kidney disease and diabetes, a diet that is high in animal protein appears to 'weaken' the kidneys, which begin to filter at a slower and less efficient rate. However, eating soya protein instead of animal protein seems to improve kidney function.

The Chinese eat soya beans in the form of soya milk, boiled or sautéed soya beans, and tofu in its many varieties, seasoned by soya sauce. Western pharmaceutical companies have isolated and extracted the key beneficial ingredients from the soya bean, concentrated them in tablet or powder form and offered them for sale as pills or food supplements. These are now available as Nature's Plus Ultra Isoflavone 100; or Solgar Iso-Soy Powder. While the latter is better than nothing, I recommend adding as many of the natural forms of soya as possible to your daily diet in order to prevent disease and maintain health. Both tofu and fresh soya beans are quite delicious and very easy to prepare.

Another staple of the Chinese diet is tea. Next to water, tea is the most popular drink in China. Tea (called *cha* 茶 in

Chinese) was first cultivated during the Han dynasty (206 BC–AD 220) and became popular among the rich in the Tang dynasty (AD 618–906). From then on, the habit spread across the land. By the eighteenth century the British had also acquired a taste for tea-drinking and were importing increasing amounts – up to 30 million pounds per year in the 1830s. In order to improve the balance of trade, Britain started exporting opium from India to China. Eventually, this opium trade led to the Opium War between China and Britain in 1842. By the 1880s British tea imports had risen to 150 million pounds per year.

Recent scientific studies reveal that leaves from the common Chinese tea-plant, *Camellia sinensis*, contain certain potent antioxidants known as polyphenols, which may help to prevent heart disease and cancer. There are three types of tea: green, oolong and black. Green tea is made by quickly steaming the freshly plucked green leaves; whereas both oolong and black teas are made by fermenting and air-drying the leaves (thereby causing oxidation which causes the leaves to turn brown or black) and then crushing them. All three teas contain roughly equal amounts of protective chemicals, although their forms may differ.

A cup of tea contains approximately half as much caffeine as a cup of coffee. More importantly, its polyphenols prevent DNA and cell damage caused by free radicals. As antioxidants, these polyphenols are more potent than vitamins C or E. Tea appears to lower serum cholesterol and triglycerides,* and protect against heart disease and stroke. In animal studies, polyphenols have been shown to ward against the development of rheumatoid arthritis and skin cancers, as well as cancers of the mouth and digestive tract. Further experiments are being carried out on humans.

---

* Triglycerides are breakdown products of fat and are harmful to the body.

My Aunt Baba was an inveterate tea drinker. She always kept a thermos of hot water and a small jar of *long jing* 龍井 (dragon's well) green tea from Hang Zhou in our room. One of my earliest memories is that of my aunt waking me at the crack of dawn on the mornings when I was scheduled to sit for important tests. She would wipe my face with a hot, moist towel and make me sit up in bed. Then she would hand me a fragrant cup of steaming green tea while she quizzed me on my home-work.

As I sat sipping my tea, bleary-eyed and half-asleep, I would watch her flipping through the pages of my textbooks with a frown of concentration, hoping and dreading to trip me up at the same time. I did not know then that these were special moments which I would treasure for the rest of my life. I longed to snuggle back under the quilt but dared not even protest because I was well aware that my aunt hated getting up early and was only doing it for me.

Whenever I made a mistake in my answers, she would urge me to take another sip of tea, think hard and try again. 'Tea sharpens the mind, soothes the stomach and nourishes your *qi*! Remember this!'

Yes! I never forgot! Especially her unwavering belief in me and the feeling that I must never let her down. Even today, getting up at 5 a.m. to sit in front of my computer while reading a scientific paper stating that tea contains polyphenols which help prevent cancer and chronic heart disease, I see her eyes poring anxiously over my printouts. 'Don't worry! Don't worry!' I tell her, over and over. 'I won't disappoint you! One day, you'll be proud of me. I promise.'

Do Chinese herbs work? Some do and some don't. Tea and tofu have long been regarded in China as *bu* (healing and restorative). Ginger brings symptomatic relief against nausea and vomiting. The opium poppy has been used to relieve pain and treat gastro-intestinal diseases such as cholera for many centuries. The versatile ginseng is said to increase a person's *yang* quality and is used to combat fatigue, build up resistance, help diabetes and prevent the negative effects of stress, especially in the elderly. Recent evidence suggests that ginseng may exert an oestrogenic as well as an adrenergic effect on the body. For over 2000 years *Ginkgo biloba* has been prescribed in China to 'benefit the brain'. Today, there is increasing evidence that ginkgo improves memory in senile forgetfulness. Recently, a company called Pharmanex Inc. has successfully extracted *cholestin* from a strain of red yeast (monascus) that is used as a flavouring and colouring agent in Chinese cooking. Cholestin contains lovastatin (the same lovastatin that is in Mevacor, an FDA-approved cholesterol-lowering drug available on prescription). The Chinese have used red yeast for many years as a nutraceutical. Numerous clinical studies done in China support the claim that cholestin lowers cholesterol.

Examination of other traditional 'remedies', such as rhinoceros horn, bear's paw and tiger's penis, has shown no evidence for their alleged claims. Rhinoceros horn has traditionally been used as a cure for impotence. Chinese herbalists in Hong Kong tell me that demand for the horn has fallen dramatically since the introduction of Viagra.

Recently, I have been invited to join the boards of three well-known universities, one of which is starting a special centre to investigate 'complementary alternate medicine'. I hope to become more knowledgeable in this complex and fascinating field.

In the late 1920s, when my father was twenty-one and living in Tianjin, he made his fortune buying the common plant *ma huang* 麻黃 (which grew in abundance in the surrounding countryside) and selling it to pharmaceutical companies in Europe and the USA. The drug ephedrine, extracted from the stem and branches of *ma huang* (known as *Ephedra sinica* in the west), is used to treat colds, influenza, asthma, hay fever, bronchitis and low blood pressure. When I worked as an anaesthesiologist in California from 1968 to 1994, I used to inject ephedrine fairly frequently into patients whose blood pressure had fallen after epidural anaesthesia. Breaking open a glass ampoule of the drug always gave me a small jolt of pride, as if I were personally responsible for its powers. Father once told me that *ma huang* had been used as a medicine in China for over 4000 years and that he himself had played a key role in the plant's export to the west. Many of the business letters dealing with the sale of *ma huang* to the largest pharmaceutical companies in the world were banged out with one finger by my teenaged father. He used to type them after dinner on a rickety second-hand typewriter, with his family clustered around in awed admiration.

Here in the west, people are gradually becoming aware of the importance of food in the maintenance of health. More and more are agreeing with the Chinese view that food and medicine should not be perceived as separate. Whatever we put in our mouths will eventually affect our bodies in one way or another. Eating a healthy diet is our first line of defence against disease and a potent form of preventive medicine. The choice and preparation of our meals are more important than anything else we might do to care for ourselves. Every month, we women spend hours at the beauty parlour and hundreds of dollars on cosmetics to improve our appearance. Unless we have a healthy body, however, such endeavour (though commendable) is unfortunately rather like applying a new coat of paint to a car with a damaged transmission. Perhaps we should simply always keep in mind the Chinese proverb: 'Yi shi wei liao' (Let food be medicine).

8

Know the Opposite Party as Well as You Know Yourself

知己知彼

ZHI JI ZHI BI

When the Chinese Communists won the civil war against the Nationalists in 1949, I was eleven years old. My parents fled to Hong Kong and abandoned me in a convent school in Tianjin, where I was the only student. Luckily Aunt Reine, my stepmother's elder sister, remembered me a few days before her own escape. She rescued me and brought me with her to Hong Kong.

Although my parents took me in and allowed me to stay, I knew in my heart that I was there on sufferance. To them, I was a nuisance and they simply did not want me around. Every day my stepmother would take Aunt Reine and her children sightseeing, leaving me at home. Secretly, I was very pleased because it was the only time I could relax and not be on tenterhooks. Besides, my grandfather frequently chose to stay home too and this gave me an opportunity to talk to him.

One morning he complained that I was forgetting my Chinese. After launching a tirade about the subtleties of our native tongue, he told me about the origins of one of his favourite characters, *bei* 貝.

'In ancient times,' he said, 'cowrie shells were used as units of money and exchanged for goods and services. In time, a hole was drilled in these shells and a row of shells was held together by a string. Look at the character *bei* carefully. Does it not resemble a row of shells held together by a piece of string knotted at the end?

'Because the word evolved from something "valuable", many later Chinese words containing the component *bei* are associated with finance or commerce in some way. Let me draw for you a maze made up of two characters, *tan* 貪 (greed) and *pin* 貧 (poverty). Place them side by side, study them and note their resemblance. At a quick glance you might even mistake one for the other. They are indeed closely linked. If you're careless and enter the web of *tan*, you will be ensnared and end up in the convolutions of *pin*. Remember: all covet, all lose.

'Take another word, *mei* 買, which means "to buy", and the word *mei* 賣, which means "to sell". Place these two words side by side – *mei mei* 買賣 – and the term means "buy/sell"; it also signifies "transaction" or "business".

'What a fantastic expression! Buy/sell! How subtle and ingenious! How profound and all-encompassing! Though the two words may appear simple and elementary, they actually encapsulate an ocean of meaning and substance. You may find it hard to believe, but these two words hold the secret to all the relationships in the world. They sound similar except for their intonation. They look the same except for the symbol *tu* 土 (dirt or land) on top of *mei* 賣 (sell). The essence of business – any business – is making buy/sell 做買賣 (*zuo mei mei*). You hope to buy low and sell high. Otherwise you will be in big trouble.

'Gradually, I have come to realise that not only business, but every relationship (whether between husband and wife, parent and child, friend and friend, colleague and colleague, employer and employee, teacher and pupil, city and city, or even nation and nation) is based on our ancient Chinese concept of buy/sell. From children playing with marbles to diplomats exchanging threats as well as couples fighting over money, the principle is identical. Underlying it all is the eternal question: Am I getting my fair share? Is what I'm receiving equivalent to what I'm giving or am I being taken advantage of? When all is said and done, did I win or lose? Which party had to "eat the loss" (吃虧 *chi kui*) or take the blame?

'If the transaction is perceived by either party as lopsided or unfair, if one side has to "eat losses" too many times, the buy/ sell will fail and the relationship will eventually end. It's as simple as that.'

Over the years I have often pondered on the wisdom of my grandfather's words in my own business dealings. I have attempted to see the buy/sell equation from the other side as well as from my own. In selling a house, if I demand an increase in my selling price, should I offer to put on a new roof? If I ask for more time before completing the transaction, should I agree to paint the doors?

It is interesting to note that in forming real-estate partnerships, American businessmen often incorporate a standard 'buy/ sell agreement' when drawing up the contract. Should the partners decide to separate at some time in the future, the buy/sell agreement would provide a fair and equitable way of accomplishing this. Since buildings cannot be physically divided, the agreement calls for one party to name a price and for the other party to decide whether he wishes to buy or to sell. In principle, this price should represent an amount that will satisfy both parties equally. The buyer ends up with the entire property while the seller pockets all the cash. Recently, I was told that another name for this type of buy/sell agreement is the 'Chinese solution' because the concept originated in China.

In personal relationships, I have become aware of certain special nuances that come into play when men and women relate to each other because men are by nature *yang* whereas women are *yin*. By merging the two Chinese concepts of *yin/yang* and *mei/mei* (buy/sell), and using my past as an illustration, I hope to bring about a better understanding of the corollaries connecting these entities so that men and women can interact with each other more harmoniously.

As I explained earlier (see page 20), the *yin/yang* concept goes far back into antiquity and is mentioned in the *I Ching*. Its influence has been extensive and profound, affecting every aspect of Chinese culture and civilisation, including art, philosophy, medicine and government. The doctrine teaches that all events come about as the result of two forces: *yin* (which is female, passive, weak and negative) and *yang* (which is male, active, strong and positive). However, *yin* and *yang* are not opposites but complement each other to maintain cosmic order. An object is intrinsically neither *yin* nor *yang* but is classified according to the role it plays relative to a second object. Thus, man is classified as *yang* in relation to the earth, but as *yin* in relation to Heaven. *Yin/yang* are two faces of the same coin. Not only can one not exist without the other, they might even change into one another. For example, summer (*yang*) gradually changes into winter (*yin*) and vice versa. Life itself is perceived as a cycle of constant change merging spontaneously from *yin* to *yang* to *yin* to *yang* and so on in perpetuity. In the symbol representing *yin/yang*, *yin* has a little dot of *yang*, while *yang* has a little dot of *yin*. Does not every male possess a little femininity and every female a little masculinity?

In Chinese gardens as well as landscape paintings, *yin* and *yang* are balanced to maintain harmony. A pool of water or a level plane of earth are *yin*. This is balanced by a *yang* hill or limestone rock jutting into the sky. Landscape paintings are named *shan shui* 山水 (mountain and water). The name itself symbolises a harmoniously balanced *yin/yang* pair.

Maintenance of health is also seen in *yin/yang* terms. Traditional Chinese medicine aims to establish a state of balance between one's body and the environment as well as a harmonious relationship between the body's various components. Illness happens when this balance becomes disturbed. In contrast to the west, where illness is *treated* with pills and injections, there is no distinction between food and medicine in Chinese thinking and the patient is merely told to *chi* 吃 (eat) his herbal concoction as part of his meals. Foods, as well as diseases, are also divided into *yin/yang* varieties. *Yin* foods such as turnips and dandelions are eaten for *yang* conditions such as pimples or oral ulcers which are thought to be caused by heat (*re qi*). *Yang* foods such as ginger and ginseng are eaten to control diarrhoea, nausea and fatigue which are all supposedly caused by *yin* factors such as a cold wind, an iced drink, or a deficient diet. A physician's task is to restore the patient's equanimity.

In Chapter One I reported my Aunt Baba's predictions: 'The pendulum of history will swing from the *yin* ashes brought by the Cultural Revolution to the *yang* phoenix arising from its wreckage.' Perhaps it is this conviction that nothing is permanent but change itself that gives us Chinese our stoicism and passive acceptance of life's misfortunes. When I saw my aunt in Shanghai in 1979, her living conditions could not have been more deplorable. Yet she had not the slightest doubt that things would soon change for the better because of the inexorable cyclical *yin/yang* transformation of human affairs.

In Amy Tan's wonderful novel *The Joy Luck Club* there is one episode which encapsulates the blending of the *yin/yang* principle with the buy/sell concept. In the chapter entitled 'Rice Husband' a mother pays a visit to her daughter and son-in-law. The daughter is anxious to hide from her mother the truth about her deteriorating marriage. Suddenly, the mother notices a grocery list stuck on the refrigerator door. On closer examination, the list appears to be carefully divided into 'his' and 'her' columns, with the exact cost of each item recorded separately. It dawns on the mother that her daughter is paying half the grocery bills even though her salary is only a fraction of her husband's.

Later that evening the daughter picks a fight with her husband. She is deeply unhappy and says, 'We need to think about what our marriage is really based on . . . not this balance sheet, who owes who what.'

Her distress is, of course, caused by the unfairness of her marital relationship. Over the years she has had to *chi kui* 'eat losses' too many times. She is unable to verbalise this, but the buy/sell is failing. She feels that she is being short-changed, not only in terms of money, but also in time, devotion, attention, courtesy, affection and loyalty. The marriage is headed for divorce.

Looking back with the wisdom of age and hindsight at the two failed relationships of my life, I cannot help but be amazed at my own crass stupidity. Did I ever really believe that I could live 'happily ever after' with either Karl or my first husband, Byron? Was I truly that naive? But of course!

When I think of Karl, my most vivid memories are of his ethereal, tenuous and achingly beautiful letters – even in hindsight and after so many years have passed. As I recall those far-off student days, the whole affair takes on a surrealistic, dream-like quality. The image of Karl – professorial, intellectual, golden, unalterable and forever thirty-four – is a larger-than-life mirage stencilled in my imagination that may never have actually existed in real life.

I remember climbing the narrow, steep stairs to his dusty and gloomy fourth-floor flat in Bloomsbury. There, freed for a few hours from the prying eyes of his colleagues and my classmates, we would huddle on rare Sunday afternoons and defer for a brief spell our mutual panics and fears. He was my first love and I was simply dumb-founded by the intoxicating enchantment of being courted by such an eminent scientist and dazzling intellect.

Oh, what recollections! There seems so much to think back upon! My youth, daring and fervour; his caution, ambivalence and withdrawal. When did I become convinced that we were doomed? Of our relationship's inevitable demise? Of the end of hope? My love was like a hallucinating fever, a labyrinth through which I hurtled, a maze without exits, a prison of anguish from which there was no escape.

Day after day, month after month, year after year, I swallowed dose after dose of *kui* or losses in our buy/sell relationship. Between any two people, the measure of affection given or received is seldom exactly equal. One side always cares more (or less) than the other. In our case, it was always I who gave in first, who made the initial phone call after a quarrel, who waited outside Karl's lab to hand him a note of apology, who begged him to take a few hours off to celebrate his birthday. I knew in my heart that his work would always come before me. He often resented the time he spent with me because it took him away from his experiments. I knew this and tried not to mind, but the *kui* losses accumulated and began to rankle inside. Perhaps my childhood experiences made my yearning for his love so intense that I persisted against all logic. I was incredibly lucky to come across my grandfather's copy of the *I Ching* at that crucial juncture in my life. As the writer Shen Gua wrote during the Northern Song dynasty (960–1126), 'Since our mind is often unavoidably burdened, at times we should substitute something that does not have a mind in order to gain access to it.'

When I finally cut loose and tore up his letters, I felt dazed but free. I thought I was whole but inside I was clogged with the dregs of seven years of rejection and denial. My tenuous sense of self-worth had been seriously undermined but I remained artlessly unaware.

A year later I met and married Byron, a Chinese engineer, after a courtship of six weeks. Why did I do this? I hardly knew. We were ill-suited and all wrong for each other. I had probably married him for the most practical reasons: companionship, children, emotional security and social acceptance. I met Byron on the very day of my arrival in New York: I had just escaped from seven years with Karl, at the end of which (no matter how I rationalised it) I had been cast aside. I was yearning for a new beginning in a new country. And there he was: the handsome hero of all the *kung fu* novels pledging eternal devotion and asking for my hand less than twenty-four hours after he set eyes on me. In a rare reflective moment shortly after the wedding, I calculated that the time Byron and I had spent alone together before our marriage amounted to less than ten hours.

Our union was doomed to failure from the beginning. We had nothing in common. In contrast to Karl, I never loved Byron. Despite his good looks and fine physique, I felt a profound indifference towards him. Whenever he touched me, I turned into stone.

Our son Roger was born a year and a half later. When Roger was six months old, Byron began beating the two of us.

Did I play a part in my own assault? Am I partially to blame for the failure of my first marriage? Was I 'swept away' by Byron out of some unrecognised neurotic needs of my own? I'm afraid the answer is 'yes' to all the above.

Why did I not walk away immediately when Byron first became physically abusive? After all, I was educated and had a secure job as an anaesthesiologist. Strange as it may seem, without admitting any of this even to myself at that time, I must have considered the buy/sell equation of our marital relationship to be still operative despite his violence.

From then on, the threat of brute force hung over our household. I could no longer sleep with Byron but I did not leave. My career as a physician had taken off and my income was substantially higher than his. That fact probably added to his resentment of me. He expected me to have a full-time career, and take care of the baby as well as all the household chores. Everything that went wrong in the house was my responsibility. At first we pooled our salaries, but after a failed business venture on his part, he banked his pay-cheques separately and used my earnings to settle all the bills.

I endured it all because I could not bear the shame of divorce and the subsequent dishonour it would bring on my family. My longing for my parents' love was so strong that I simply dared not tell them the truth. At the hospital I made up stories to explain my black eyes and bruises to the nurses and other medical colleagues, feeling embarrassed, foolish and ashamed.

Things might have gone on like this for the rest of my life if my parents had not paid us a visit when I was in the sixth year of my dismal marriage. After staying the weekend with us, they must have sensed that our union was troubled. This is how I describe it in my book *Falling Leaves*.

My father, stepmother and I were by ourselves when I drove them back to their hotel . . .

'The block of apartments you showed us two days ago,' Father said, 'the one you are thinking of buying. Whose name will be on the deed as the legal owner?'

'I have put both Byron's and my name down as the buyers, Father,' I answered truthfully. 'This is the way it's done in America. When we bought our house, it was also purchased in our joint names.'

'What you are doing is unwise and will lead to complications,' Father admonished, 'Zhong gua de gua (種瓜得瓜 You plant melons, you reap melons). When Byron was in Hong

Kong, he and his father told us they had bought a property in Kowloon. Is your name on the deed there?'

I faltered, shocked. 'I don't think so, Father. Byron never asked me to sign any papers.' The conversation was veering painfully close to a discussion about the state of my marriage.

'Then why are you putting his name on your apartments when he has not contributed one cent towards their purchase? Don't be naive, Adeline! Don't think you are above these money matters, because you are not. Consult a good lawyer and make sure the property is in your name and your name alone. Do you hear?'

I had been 'eating losses' (*chi kui*) continuously for the six years of our marriage because of my innate feelings of unworthiness. Deep inside, I was still the scared little girl who was afraid of being rejected. Secretly, I had hoped that by constantly 'letting him win', I would enable Byron to undergo a miraculous trans-formation; he would come to love me even though I didn't believe I was really good enough to be loved. Although I knew that Byron was self-centred and headstrong, I still thought he had other virtues like integrity and honesty. But the moment my father pointed out Byron's deviousness in purchasing his Hong Kong property behind my back, a balance tipped over somewhere inside me. The marital buy/sell was no longer oper-ative and our marriage was over.

If we merge the *yin/yang* principle with the buy/sell equation in male/female relationships and acknowledge that men are largely (but not entirely) *yang* and differ from women, who are mostly (though not totally) *yin*, then we ought to accept that these differences should be understood, remembered and acted upon by both sides in order to maintain a durable and happy partnership.

Portrait of Yin

More than anything else, *Yin* needs to communicate. *Yin* yearns to have frequent meaningful dialogues, and be understood. Unburdening her problems and revealing herself to *Yang* is vitally important to *Yin*.

Respect Yin*'s fundamental need. Listen to* Yin, *look at her, and hold her if necessary. Often,* Yang *does not even have to reply, he can just nod and look sympathetic. Why? Because* Yin *is searching primarily for emotional support and validation, only secondarily for logical answers.*

Yin likes to make frequent small complaints which are repetitive and annoying. What *Yang* needs to remember is that when *Yin* complains, she is mostly sharing her feelings and seeking relief from stress, not asking for solutions or casting blame.

Yang *should keep in mind that the complaints are not directed at him.* Yin *is simply blowing off steam. Whether or not* Yang *agrees with her sentiments, he should try to give her the emotional support she is looking for at that moment. Choose another, calmer time to have a problem-solving conversation.*

Yin has a burning desire to help *Yang*. She yearns for *Yang* to improve and advance. In the process, *Yin* may advise *Yang* to stop smoking, drink less, eat more vegetables, exercise, phone his mother, send birthday cards to his boss, etc.

Yang *dislikes this intensely but he should try not to feel hostile.* Yang *must not perceive* Yin*'s constant nagging as her attempt to criticise and control him. Instead,* Yang *should remind himself* *that this is* Yin*'s way of expressing her love for him.* Yin *wishes to improve* Yang *and nags because she cares.*

Yin has monthly mood swings brought about by her body's hormonal fluctuations. Yin's periods can be excruciatingly painful, like attacks of severe stomach-ache. These may wake Yin up from a sound sleep and go on for twenty-four hours. When Yin gets older and goes through menopause, she might become depressed, irrational or even suicidal. Yang needs to remember that Yin's symptoms are real and not a figment of her imagination.

Yang *should not dismiss* Yin*'s symptoms as 'nothing'. Instead,* Yang *should try to give* Yin *the support that she craves for, hold her if she clings to him, dry her tears if she weeps and try not to scold or ask for explanations.*

When upset, Yin needs to talk. When the video-recorder or the computer malfunctions, Yin turns to anyone and everyone for help. When lost, Yin asks for directions from strangers. All these are Yin's instincts that form part of her nature. When Yin is with Yang, she may forget that she is not alone and end up manifesting the same behaviour.

Yang *should not take it as a personal insult if* Yin *suddenly walks away from him and starts requesting help from the idiot who lives across the hall, while* Yang *is desperately searching for clues in the operation manual of her new computer.* Yang *shouldn't have an epileptic seizure simply because* Yin *is asking for directions from a passing car while* Yang *is driving at high speed and trying to find the way to* Yin*'s mother's new house. To* Yin, *seeking help is not a sign of weakness or a defect. It is simply* Yin*'s way and she certainly did not do it to humiliate* Yang.

Yin expects Yang to remember her birthday, their wedding anniversary and major holidays. She gets very hurt if he forgets. She is a gatherer and enjoys strolling from store to store looking at the merchandise. She would rather talk on the phone with a friend or read a book than watch the boxing match on television.

Daily small tokens of Yang's *affection will mean more to* Yin *than the occasional grand gesture of jewellery or fur. Cook for* Yin. *Take out the garbage. Tell* Yin *of his devotion. Reassure* Yin *and make her feel safe.*

Profile of Yang

Yang is a practical creature. When troubled, *Yang* prefers to ponder and solve his problems alone. The last thing *Yang* wants is to admit failure or communicate his distress. *Yang* is searching for down-to-earth solutions, not sympathy or verbal assurance.

Respect Yang *and give him the space that he needs. Even if* Yin *is dying of curiosity, she should not bombard* Yang *with questions.* Yin *should tell* Yang *that she accepts, trusts and loves him. After that, speak no more and leave* Yang *alone. When* Yang *is ready, he will open up to* Yin.

Yang is goal-oriented, not people-oriented. *Yang* is more interested in furthering his career, building his house, learning to fly and inventing new gadgets than in meeting people or making new friends. *Yang* does not enjoy long phone conversations. *Yang* phones his buddies for a purpose, then hangs up; whereas *Yin* phones her friends to 'catch up and network' and have meandering, nurturing conversations.

Give Yang *the support as well as the space that he craves for. Divide domestic chores in such a way as to take into account each partner's likes and dislikes.* Yang *usually prefers carpentry, car-washing, fixing gadgets or sweeping the side-walk; whereas* Yin *favours cooking, sewing, flower arrangements and socialising over the phone.*

Yang tends to concentrate on his career outside the home and leave domestic and social decisions to *Yin*. Unless reminded, *Yang* will forget to attend his children's school performances, send birthday greetings to his mother, or visit his old college room-mate who is laid up in the hospital. (For the first fourteen years of my life, I meant so little to my successful and prosperous father that he even forgot my Chinese name, a name he himself had given me at birth.) *Yang* considers his children 'extensions' of himself, and only remembers them when the children have done something extraordinary and commendable. Although *Yang* loves his children, his nature directs him to concentrate his time and energy on his job.

Yin *should try not to be too hurt if* Yang *forgets their wedding anniversary or her birthday. That's how* Yang*'s mind works and his forgetfulness is not a reflection of his feelings for* Yin. *Remind* Yang *to phone his mother on Mother's Day and to come home early for the children's piano recital. Social niceties are not* Yang*'s forte. Though* Yang *is no good at phoning and inviting friends for a dinner party, he is often the life and soul of the party once it is organised by* Yin.

If the couple is invited out for dinner at eight o'clock, *Yang* will be ready and waiting in the car at 7.30 p.m., dressed in the same dark-blue suit he has worn like a uniform for the last four years. For recreation, *Yang* yearns to be a 'hunter' (at least in his imagination) and enjoys watching ball games or boxing matches on television, identifying himself with the champion.

Yin *is irritated that* Yang *is already waiting in the car while she is still in the shower, talking over the phone, or racking her brain to find a dress that no one has seen before. Something in* Yang *makes him want to be punctual (even a little early), but* Yin *'knows' she never wants to be the first to arrive. Although she cannot understand how* Yang *can watch television sports hour after hour, she should accept that this is his way of relaxing and it is important to him.*

Yang's nature makes him wish to project an image of himself as competent, powerful and efficient. When things go badly at work, *Yang* becomes moody and withdrawn at home. Instead of confiding in *Yin* and his children, *Yang* ignores them and shuts himself in his study, trying to figure a way out and find the answer on his own.

This is not the time to question, advise, analyse or criticise. Yang's *silence does not mean he doesn't love* Yin. Yang's *nature makes him wish to be left alone at such times and* Yin *should respect* Yang's *wish for solitude. However,* Yang *needs* Yin's *love and acceptance, now more than ever.* Yin *must let* Yang *know that she is there for him if he needs her.* Yin *should cook* Yang *his favourite foods or buy him small gifts to show that she cares. However,* Yin *should offer suggestions only if* Yang *turns to her for advice.*

At all times, keep in mind that underlying it all, the buy/sell equation is perpetually in operation. To some extent, every relationship is transactional and each side keeps a mental scorecard of what is given versus what is received, what is 'bought' and what is 'sold'. Though at any one time, one side or another may try to justify a certain action, each partner knows in his or her heart exactly how the land lies and what the score is. Being fairly treated is a fundamental human desire present in everyone.

In serious relationships between men and women it is important for both sides to be considerate and to give way to the other as much as possible. The Chinese word *ran* 讓 expresses this sentiment very well. It means to 'give in', 'make way', 'step aside' or 'concede'.

Occasional conflict is unavoidable in any long-term intimate relationship. *Yin* seldom changes into *Yang*; and *Yang* is unlikely to be transformed into *Yin*. *Ran* is a complex word that incorporates the elements of acceptance, courtesy, concession and empathy towards the other party's viewpoint. Quarrels usually arise from a wish to control or change a partner's personality or behaviour. Both sides should keep in mind that the person we have most control over is not our partner but ourselves. By making a conscious effort to accept our partner and love him or her as he or she is, the relationship is more likely to turn from combat to cooperation. This is illustrated by the proverb *zhi ji zhi bi* 知己知彼 (know the opposite party as well as you know yourself).

Some couples get into the habit of lashing out at each other in the mistaken belief that by humiliating their partner, they have gained something. Unfortunately, the opposite is true. In such quarrels, not only have they won nothing, they have depleted their partner's *qi* and diminished their own.

Between friends, the buy/sell equation usually takes the form of exchanging favours. A invites B for tennis. B takes A to the airport. B fixes A's dishwasher. A helps B to write his resumé. When they go out to dinner or to a movie, A and B split the tab down the middle.

For friendship to survive, it needs to be guided with care and endowed with generosity. Both sides must also perceive the *mei/mei* as being fair. If party A feels that she is continually giving and giving without receiving sufficient (money, affection, time or favours) from B, A will eventually act out her resentment and lash out at B. In the course of our lives, we all go through different phases. As children and teenagers, most of us have many acquaintances with whom we are thrown together at school. Between the ages of twenty and thirty we start choosing as friends those with similar goals, interests, education or pursuits. From thirty to fifty we are usually too preoccupied with children, spouse and careers to cultivate new friendships. After the age of fifty, as children grow up and leave home, friendship assumes an increasing importance (in terms of happiness and emotional satisfaction) until the end.

Between parents and children, the buy/sell equation is much more complicated, unpredictable and variable, depending on individual personalities. Parents normally give their children all their money, time, love and attention 'unconditionally' when the children are small. When the children become adults, there is often a transition period during which 'children' still expect their parents to do everything and pay every bill. (I have known forty-something 'children' earning huge salaries who automatically expect their parents to pay the cheque whenever they dine together.) Most grown-up offspring, however, are kind, gentle, protective and generous towards their parents as they get older.

In my relationship with Karl, we never progressed to the point of give-and-take. Looking back, I don't think he ever seriously considered marrying me. For him, our friendship may have started off as a diversion, a fling which got out of hand. He probably never expected to be embroiled with someone so young, so intense, so committed and so obsessed. When I finally destroyed his letters and left, he was doubtless relieved.

I have always felt guilty for marrying Byron because I never loved him. During our time together I tried to make it up to him by being the super-wife, super-physician and super-mother, but unexpressed mutual discontent always bubbled beneath the surface. I felt I was giving in to him endlessly. While 'eating my losses' over and over in silence, I became increasingly withdrawn and cold. It was a relief when my parents advised me to leave him.

I met Bob a year after my divorce on a blind date arranged by a woman friend. We have been married for twenty-seven years. Right from the beginning, and throughout our time together, he has been caring and true. In the whole of my life I have never encountered anyone so loving or felt so cherished. As an anaesthesiologist, I was often called to the hospital for emergencies. Operations were stressful and frequently lasted well into the night. No matter what time I came home, however, I would find the dinner cooked and my husband waiting for me. Sometimes, he'd be so exhausted he would doze off while we ate.

After the publication of *Falling Leaves* I received many invitations to speak at public functions in different places. Without hesitation, Bob would always accompany me. Because of him, these occasions became mini-vacations rather than stressful obligations. He has heard my speeches so many times he probably knows them by heart, but he is invariably there, sitting unobtrusively in a corner doing his crossword puzzle. The knowledge of his presence is indescribably comforting and means everything in the world to me.

Every day he shows me tokens of his love. Not with words, but through his every action. In our marital buy/sell relationship I know I am continually in his debt – a debt that can never be adequately repaid.

And I am grateful.

9

Hidden Logic Within the Shape of Words

字形藏理

ZI XING CANG LI

As a six-year-old, I once asked my teacher in Shanghai why Chinese words were shaped the way they were. During a dictation test I had written the word *che* 車 incorrectly and received a bad mark. I was annoyed and wanted to know why *che* could not be written my way. My teacher responded by ordering me to copy out *che* fifty times with brush and ink.

That afternoon my grandfather quizzed me as he watched me do my extra homework. When I told him about my exchange with my teacher, he reacted differently.

'Your question is very interesting,' he told me. 'Ours is a pictorial language. Each word is a picture of an image or an idea expressed on paper. The characters look the way they do because they started off as drawings. Over time, they developed their present forms. Learning the history and early patterns of Chinese characters often reveals a fascinating story of the everyday life of our ancestors.

'The word *che* means "vehicle"' or "car". In ancient times

155

there were no motor-cars. Transportation was by carts or carriages. Turn your paper around and look at the word *che* from a different angle. Does it not look like a cart with a wheel on each side and an axle running down the middle?

'In future, when you look at any Chinese word, keep in mind the phrase *Zi xing cang li* 字形藏理 (Hidden logic within the shape of words). *Li* means logic, reason, truth and principle. Dissect each word and search for the *li* represented by the characters.

'For example, how we Chinese regard the ant might be seen by looking at the word for "ant" 蟻 (*yi*). On the left is 虫, which means "insect". On the right is 義, which means "justice, loyalty, relationship and unselfishness".'

Of all the animals, only we humans are endowed with the ability to communicate through language. Described by philosophers as a 'mirror of man's mind', language reflects the essence of our perceptions and concepts. We use it to clarify our thoughts, feelings or ideas and express them to others.

Ideas define how we perceive reality. At first glance, having ideas may seem to be a natural function separate from the domain of language. Indeed, in some instances, it is. Although it is mainly through words that we express our ideas, it is by no means the only way.

Emotional and spiritual concepts are probably best conveyed by music, art, meditation or physical disciplines such as dance, *qi gong*, *tai chi* or yoga. A skilful artist is able to erase the boundary between observation, feeling and expression, thereby creating a conduit directly to the mind of the beholder.

Ideas in mathematics, however, are better interpreted by a special numerical 'alphabet' that is able to represent an infinite variety of concepts with a small and simple assemblage of symbols. Galileo wrote,

> Philosophy is written in that great book which ever lies before our eyes – I mean the universe. But we cannot understand it [the universe] if we do not first learn the language and grasp the symbols in which it is written. This book [of the universe] is written in the mathematical language, and the symbols are triangles, circles, and other geometrical figures, without whose help it is impossible to comprehend a single word of it, without which one wanders in vain through a dark labyrinth.

The way in which we think – and the degree of sophistication of the culture we create – is highly dependent on our vocabulary. The importance of mathematics in the development of science was recognised by the Chinese only relatively recently, and the Hindu-Arabic number system was not adopted or taught at schools in China until the twentieth century. Yet according to Leonardo da Vinci, 'a science is perfect to the degree that it is mathematical'. In the 1880s, when my grandfather was a boy, numbers were still being written in Chinese characters with a brush. Besides being cumbersome and time-consuming, the traditional Chinese method of recording numbers lacked two vital components: *positional value* and the symbol *zero*.

When my son Roger was seven years old, I gave him a record called *Multiplication Rock*, which he loved. Morning, noon and night he would play it over and over, driving our whole family crazy with the same tunes, same beat, same words. One of the songs was named 'My Hero Zero'. It went something like this:

My hero Zero,
When you stand to the right of the number one
The number becomes ten;
When you stand to the right of the number ten
The number becomes one hundred;
When you stand to the right of the number one hundred
The number becomes one thousand.

Roger loved the song so much that, for his eighth birthday, I wrote him a short story featuring his hero Zero (dressed in a bright red military uniform) coming to the rescue of all the other nine numbers which had mocked and belittled him for being of no value.

In a way, this story symbolises the reason why China fell behind the west in mathematics and science. The symbol zero, invented in India in the ninth century and adopted as part of the Hindu-Arabic number system, is indeed very much a hero. However, zero's value was never truly recognized by my Chinese ancestors before the twentieth century.

For one thing, zero is different from any other number. Like the mysterious, ineffable *tao* in Lao Zi's *Tao Te Ching*, zero

. . . resembles an empty bowl
Which, while being used, can never be filled.
Bottomless, it seems to be the source of everything.
Blunting all sharpness,

Unravelling all complications,
Harmonising all glare,
Uniting the world into common dust.
Hidden and invisible,
Yet it appears to exist.
I know not whose offspring it is;
It looks like the ancestor of all.

Before its invention, zero played a hidden role as a blank space on the abacus. Its incarnation as a symbol (and its establishment as a place-holder) is what gave zero its unique power and status. I have been fascinated by zero ever since I studied it as a schoolgirl in Hong Kong. Trying to discover the logic hidden within its shape (*zi xing cang li*), I became bewitched and enchanted. I was taught that adding a number to zero or subtracting zero from a number changed nothing. In such cases, zero counted for naught. However, any number *multiplied* by zero became zero itself, whereas any number *divided* by zero became infinity. I remember being thrilled by zero's paradoxical powers, seemingly so insignificant. To me at the age of twelve, zero and infinity, like *yin* and *yang*, or nothing and eternity, appeared to represent the two opposite ends of the universe. Between them, they held all the secrets of a magical world.

My feelings towards zero have not changed over the years. Like the *tao*, zero will always remain enigmatic and beautiful.

Indian astronomical tables were first translated into Arabic in Baghdad and later into Latin. The great scholar and intellectual Pope Silvester II (who was pontiff for only four years, from AD 999 to 1003) was one of the earliest proponents of these numbers, but it was Leonardo Fibonacci of Pisa (1170–1230) who, in his book *Liber Abace,* first pointed out zero's

159

unique significance. He also noted that the ten Hindu-Arabic numbers (987654321 and zero) possess the ability to express an infinite variety of numbers.

Four centuries later, Leibniz, while reading the *I Ching*, recognised that, instead of using ten numbers, any number can also be written by using only zero and 1. This is the binary (base 2) system of mathematics that is used in computers today. To Leibniz, one stood for God, zero stood for the void and binary mathematics symbolised the creation of the universe out of nothing (*Creation ex nibilo*). In 1703 he published an article in the French Academy of Sciences discussing the relationship between binary mathematics and the *I Ching*. His correspondence with the Jesuit missionaries Bouvet, Foucquet and Gaubil showed an intense desire to learn from Chinese thought and philosophy.

The advantages of using Hindu-Arabic numerals were so manifest that they gradually replaced all other number systems. They have now been accepted internationally as *the* basic 'alphabet' in the language of mathematics, called by some the 'one and only truly universal language'. Though the same numbers and mathematical symbols are pronounced differently in different countries, their meanings remain the same throughout the world. This has greatly facilitated the advancement and exchange of scientific knowledge.

As mentioned before, the invention of zero simultaneously introduced the other key concept that produced such a revolution in mathematical thought. That concept is known as 'position'.

The great eighteenth-century mathematician Laplace said of position, 'The idea is so simple that this very simplicity is the reason for our not being sufficiently aware how much admiration it deserves.'

These two inventions (positional value of a digit and the symbol for zero) are considered by many to be among the most important developments in mathematics in the last 3000 years. Zero allows every number to be put in its rightful place. The number 2 in front of three zeros (2000) has an entirely different value from the same number 2 in front of six (2,000,000) or nine (2,000,000,000) zeros. Each given number could be considered to have two values: a fundamental value indicated by the isolated numeral itself, and a place value dependent on the numeral's location within the sequence of digits used to express a particular number.

China invented the abacus (*suan pan* 算盤) or counting board in the sixth century BC and continued to use it for the next 2500 years. There is an implied understanding of both positional value and the concept of zero whenever a number is 'registered' on the abacus. For instance, the number 1001 involves placing a single disc in the fourth box from the right, leaving the third and second boxes empty to signify zeros, and putting another single disc in the first box. However, when this same number was written down as Chinese characters, it was transcribed as *yi qian yi* 一千一 (one thousand one).

But like old Roman numerals, the three words *yi qian yi* possess neither place value nor the symbol for zero. This meant that Chinese mathematicians were unable to transpose numbers on to paper quickly and easily for accurate calculation. Mathematical thought lacked an adequate alphabet for expression, progression or development. As a result, calculus was never invented, the development of science was hindered and China fell behind the west in technology.*

* Note: According to Robert Temple in *The Genius of China* (1986), the zero symbol first appeared in print in China in 1247. However, the Chinese were secretive and seldom published their work. It was also traditional not to reveal step-by-step calculations in solving mathematical problems.

If one compares the writings of Marco Polo (1254–1324), describing the Yuan dynasty, with those of Matteo Ricci (1552–1610), who was in China during the Ming dynasty, the differences are astonishing. Marco Polo's *The Book of Marco Polo* is filled with the might, power and marvels (printing, paper money, grand canals) of a rich and amazingly advanced country, while Matteo Ricci's *China in the Sixteenth Century* describes a nation ignorant of physics, geometry and astronomy; one whose people suffered from illiteracy and superstition and practised foot-binding and female infanticide. Far from being in awe of his host-country, Ricci was attracting potential converts (including some of the best and brightest scholar-mandarins) by dazzling them with European clocks, prisms, telescopes, globes, maps, paintings and books on mathematics and astronomy. In a period of less than 300 years the west had caught up with and surpassed China in science and technology.

During the summer of 1951, when I was thirteen, my stepmother allowed me to come home for a few days to recuperate from pneumonia (see page 90). My brother James had just escaped from China to Hong Kong and was sharing a room with my grandfather. They placed a cot between their two beds and the three of us would talk deep into the night, with James and me bombarding Ye Ye with questions about his past. His life as a boy in the city of Nantao, Shanghai, during the Qing dynasty fascinated me.

'What was it like, wearing a queue?' I asked one night.

'My older brothers used to tease me by tying my queue to a bed post when I was sleeping. I always hated my hairstyle but the queue was mandated by the Qing emperors and disobedience meant death by beheading. The only permitted alternative was to shave off all the hair on my head and I soon did so.'

'What was Father like as a young man?' James said.

'He was so intelligent! I remember when he first joined my firm, Hwa Chong Hong, at eighteen. He had just come to Tianjin from Shanghai and was with us for barely three months when our boss, K. C. Li, called me into his office. "This son of yours is really something!" he exclaimed. "In less than three months he has already cleared up our messy accounts and caught the thief in our midst."

'In those days, accounts were added, subtracted, multiplied or divided only by using the abacus.* Now the abacus is a wonderful instrument, but there is no written record of the steps a person goes through in arriving at his final number. In fact, it is traditional in China not to write down the sequence of calculations one goes through in solving mathematical problems. What your father did was to teach everyone the foreigners' number system and insist that everyone write down his calculations on paper one step at a time.

'For over two thousand years additions, subtractions, multiplications and divisions involving large numbers could only be carried out on the abacus because written Chinese numbers contain neither zero nor position. After learning the Hindu-Arabic numbers, young clerks at our firm were successfully challenging traditional abacists [those using the abacus] in their daily calculations. Not only were they fast and accurate, these

---

* It is possible, but highly cumbersome, to do mathematical calculations on paper while using Chinese characters alone. Until the adoption of the Hindu-Arabic number system, almost all calculations were carried out on the abacus in China out of necessity, not preference.

young followers of your father had the advantage of a permanent written record of their calculations.

'In a large firm like ours, it was easy to embezzle small sums of money and not get caught. The thief, Ho Lan, used to conveniently "convert" an occasional ten dollars into one dollar on the abacus and pocket the difference. Nobody could catch him before your father joined the firm. After that, there were no more discrepancies.'

'Who taught Father the foreign numbers, Ye Ye?' James demanded.

'I enrolled your father at Chen Tien missionary school from a young age. It was one of the most expensive Catholic boys' schools in Shanghai. There they taught him English, mathematics and science. When he graduated, he decided to get a summer job as an office boy at my firm in Tianjin before going on to university. He did so well there and was promoted so fast that he gave up his plans for higher education altogether and started his own firm two years later.'

In contrast to mathematical language, spoken language links sound with meaning. Chinese differs from English in that Chinese words are monosyllabic and there is no alphabet connecting the writing to its pronunciation. Every word is represented by a different symbol, whose sound and concept have to be separately memorised. English letters give the pronunciation while Chinese characters paint ideas and hint at thoughts.

My grandfather Ye Ye once knew a quiet Frenchman who worked as a translator at the French consulate in Shanghai. He never learned to speak Chinese and used to communicate with Ye Ye only by letter. Intelligent and artistic, he was nicknamed the 'mute calligrapher' by his Chinese staff for his sinewy handwriting, each word powerfully stroked out with a camel-hair brush, ink and lots of *qi* or energy.

When my grandfather was born in 1878, the majority of Chinese were illiterate. There was no public education and boys from wealthy families were taught by private tutors at home. Girls were not encouraged to read or write.

From the time of Confucius, China's written language had passed almost unchanged from generation to generation for 2500 years. Meanwhile, the spoken tongue developed independently. As time went on, the written classical language, known as *wen yan* 文言, diverged more and more from the spoken tongue. Although *wen yan* was a 'dead language' (like Latin) and nobody spoke it, it was the established written medium for the imperial examinations. As such, it was a symbol of power and commanded the utmost respect.

As I mentioned in the chapter on Confucius (see page 64), in 1917 Dr Hu Shih brought about a linguistic revolution called the Chinese Renaissance. The spoken vernacular was finally adopted as the written medium in place of classical Chinese, *wen yan*. New words as well as punctuation were added to reflect the living spoken tongue. For the first time in 2500 years, speech and writing became unified to create newspapers, books and magazines in a living language.

Of the 1.3 billion people in China, the majority speak Mandarin, the dialect of Beijing that is also known as *guo yu* 國語

(national language) or *pu tong hua* 普通話 (common speech). The remainder speak different dialects such as Cantonese, Shanghainese, Fukianese, etc. However, written communication is possible among all literate Chinese regardless of their native dialects because Chinese writing carries the same meaning that is independent of its pronunciation.

Chinese is the oldest living language in the world. In Dawenkon specimens of early writing were found on pottery dating back to 2597 BC. Words were also found carved on tortoise shells and ox bones from the Shang dynasty (1766–1123 BC).

There are said to be over 50,000 Chinese characters (compared to over 600,000 English words), although an average Chinese dictionary contains only around 10,000. However, knowledge of only 3500 characters will enable a reader to comprehend 99 per cent of the contents of a newspaper. Because each character has only one syllable and the actual number of different-sounding Chinese syllables is limited to 434, many characters with entirely different meanings are pronounced similarly although written differently. In Mandarin, the character for 'mother' 媽 is pronounced *ma*. *Ma* is also the pronunciation for many other words, such as 'horse' 馬, 'scold' 罵, 'numb' 麻, 'ant' 螞蟻, etc. In speaking Chinese, then, how does one distinguish one *ma* from another *ma*?

To avoid this confusion, spoken Chinese has evolved into a bisyllabic language. It is estimated that over 80 per cent of the terms used in everyday speech consists of two or more characters. Bisyllabism has been achieved by adding a second word to clarify or classify the first word.

Similar sounding words are also differentiated in speech by the use of *tones*, of which there are four to each syllable. Mastery of these tones is essential in speaking Chinese correctly. Taking the sound *ma* as our example, if it is pronounced in the first, high-keyed, explosive tone *ma* 媽 means 'mother'. Pronounced in the second, rising tone as if asking a question, *ma* 麻 means 'numb' or 'ant'. The third tone is one of curving inflection from low to high and this *ma* 馬 means 'horse'. The fourth tone is one of falling inflection and here *ma* 罵 means 'scold'.

Each Chinese character originated either from the picture of an object (such as 田 for 'farm') or from the symbol for an idea (such as 上 for 'up' and 下 for 'down'). As civilisation progressed, two or more characters were combined into a third, newly-assembled, compound character with its own pronunciation and meaning, such as two trees 林 to denote 'forest'; sun 日 above a horizontal line to denote 'dawn' 旦; strength 關係 combined with field 田 to denote 'man' 親感.

Many compound characters consist of two parts. One part is called the 'significant radical' and may convey a general idea of the category to which a particular character belongs. The other part may give a clue to its pronunciation. The word for 'mother' has a significant radical, *nu* 女 (woman), on the left, and the character 馬 (horse) on the right. Because 'horse' is pronounced *ma*, it is an indication that 'mother' 媽 is also pronounced *ma*.

Most Chinese words cannot be classified as nouns, adjectives, verbs or adverbs. The majority are 'root words' and can move from one category to another with the greatest flexibility. Like Jacks-of-all-trades, they can perform any function that is called for. Depending on its position in a sentence, a word such as *xia* (down) can be used to have the following meanings: 'to descend' (verb), 'an inferior' (noun), 'next' (adverb), 'lowly' (adjective), as well as many others.

Chinese is a non-inflectional language and its grammar is unique for its lack of rules. There are no tenses, plurals, genders or forms, cases or endings. There are also no prefixes or suffixes in Chinese. Hence it is not possible to add the letters *pre* to the word 'date' to convey the concept of 'pre-date'. Nor is it possible to add the letters 'ish' to the word 'pink' to convey the colour 'pinkish'.

The Chinese language relies almost entirely on word order (the position of a word in a sentence) and the use of auxiliary words to convey meaning. A sentence such as 'I hit he' in Chinese differs from 'He hit I' only in the position of its words. In English, a noun is a noun is a noun (to parody Gertrude Stein). To the westerner, a noun connotes a 'substance' with its own properties. But in Chinese, practically any root word can become a noun, depending on its position in a sentence. The meaning of any single word cannot be determined except in relation to the other words. Thus, in the Chinese language, word relationship is more important than the 'thing' itself.

Auxiliary words are called 'empty' words because they have no meaning in themselves. An auxiliary word such as 嗎 added at the end of a sentence is like a question mark.

It is difficult to decipher the exact meaning of a sentence when there are so few grammatical rules. Word inflection in English categorises each word in a sentence into singular or plural noun; past, present or future verb; quality of a thing or an action. But Chinese words are uninflected and their meaning cannot be deduced except in relation to other words. This results in writing that is ambiguous, imprecise, and open to widely different interpretations. Legal concepts and abstract sequences of logical reasoning, where every word counts, are sometimes difficult to translate accurately from English into Chinese.

Chinese sentences do not need to have a verb. 'Big house' is a complete sentence in Chinese. Moreover, there is no verb 'to be' in Chinese. In western thought, subject and attribute are separate. But a sentence such as 'To be or not to be' is impossible to say in Chinese (I have seen it translated as 'Let me live or let me die'). In the west existence is thought of as an independent attribute that can be added to or subtracted from a separate form. The Chinese language does not separate the two.

A simple English sentence such as 'There *is* a dog' would be translated into Chinese as '*Has* dog'. Obviously, the meaning of 'is' differs from 'has' but there is no exact Chinese equivalent to 'is'. To the Chinese mind, someone 'has' the dog, although that someone is unstated. The Chinese term 有 (has) is the only possible translation for the English word 'is' as used in this sentence, but the term 'has' implies that the dog belongs to a vague, unnamed entity whereas no such relationship is implied in the English phrase.

One common error made by Chinese people speaking English is in the use of the pronouns 'he', 'she' and 'it'. 'He' 他, 'she' 她 and 'it' 它 are all written differently in Chinese but pronounced the same: *ta*. In carrying out a conversation in English, many Chinese frequently say 'he' for 'she' or 'it' and vice versa (I have made the mistake myself). Because the sound *ta* stands for all three pronouns in Chinese, something in our brain circuitry makes us mix up these words when we speak in English, causing much confusion for our listeners.

In attempting to communicate proper nouns such as someone's name or address, we Chinese are often reduced to writing the information down on paper. At cocktail parties and social functions where pen and paper are not readily available, we resort to 'writing' out the correct sequence of strokes denoting a particular character in the air or on the hand of the listener. Where such pantomime-writing is impossible (over the telephone, for instance), we may have to resort to e-mail, fax or letter to transmit the intended words. Perhaps this is why the *way* in which words are written is so important to us.

In 1996, when *Falling Leaves* was first accepted for publication in England, my editor Susan Watt proudly presented me with a sample of a lovely book cover designed by a young British artist. It showed four photographs (of my stepmother, father, grandfather and aunt) displayed at the top, with the title *Falling Leaves* immediately below. Susan added that the four Chinese words '*Luo ye gui gen*', which means 'Falling leaves return to their roots', were being painted in abstract form and would be submitted later for my approval.

When I saw the finished cover with the Chinese words added, I became very upset. I had never realised before what a vital part calligraphy plays in my personal, emotional well-being. The artist, who was not trained in Chinese calligraphy, had given his best effort but the result was a childish scrawl, devoid of feeling, like graffiti scribbled on the surface of an abandoned building. After a sleepless night, I was able to persuade Susan to engage a learned Chinese scholar to write the words instead.

Chinese calligraphy is an art form that, ideally, evokes an emotional response at a visceral level that can never be rendered in the alphabetised Pinyin version of the same word based on sound alone. More prestigious than painting, music or poetry, *shu fa* 書法 (the art of writing) was one of the most revered forms of art in imperial China. I have seen devout Buddhists on their knees praying to a Buddha whose image was represented solely by the single Chinese word *fo* 佛 (buddha), sculpted out of the face of a hill, showing a holistic understanding that seemed to transcend psychological barriers. Somehow,

I'm unable to imagine anyone being moved to the same extent by a Pinyin (alphabetised) version of the same word.

Although there is no correlation between writing and speech in Chinese, how we speak does affect our way of thinking. Each language builds a fence around those who speak it from birth, imprisoning our thought within its vocabulary (and grammar) unless we find a way out. Freedom is achieved by becoming familiar with a second language. This new knowledge enables us to view our first language objectively from without, creating fresh insight while further enhancing the interplay between language and thought.

As a Chinese-American immigrant from China, I am frequently asked whether I feel more at home in China or in America. The truth is that when I am among Chinese people, I feel Chinese; whereas when I am among Americans, I feel American. I also know that when I switch back and forth between the two languages, my mood, expression, gestures, posture and (even) humour take on a corresponding hue.

In the winter of 1979 my Chinese-American husband Bob and I visited China with a group of Anglo-American friends. At that time the country was just beginning to admit tourists after an interval of thirty years. Everywhere we went, crowds would gather and people would stare and point at us as if we were visitors from outer space.

On our last afternoon in Shanghai our friends begged me to telephone a nearby antique store to arrange a shopping spree. It was almost 5 p.m. and they were worried that the store might close. Over the phone I was able to persuade the reluctant assistant to keep the store open after closing time provided we arrived before five.

As soon as I hung up, I ran to the store while my husband gathered together the rest of our group. The shop assistant turned out to be an unhappy-looking woman in her fifties. I was thrilled to be able to converse with her in my native Shanghai dialect and we chatted amiably for a while. I told her that I was a physician living in California.

As time went by, however, and my 'group of American friends' failed to appear, she became increasingly disgruntled and suspicious. 'You said they would be here in five minutes. It's been almost half an hour and they are still not here. My husband has the flu and I have to go home and cook dinner. Where are the Americans?'

'They'll be here any minute, I promise. It'll be worth your while because they'll buy lots of souvenirs.'

'Doesn't matter to me,' she said indifferently. 'I get the same measly salary even if they buy everything in this store. I can't wait any longer. Come back tomorrow.'

'Tomorrow we're leaving for Beijing at the crack of dawn. I can't understand why they're not here yet.'

She was rattling her keys and turning out the lights with a sour, determined look on her face.

'Come on,' I cajoled. 'They'll be here any minute. You'll make me lose face (*diu mian zi* 丢面子) if you lock up now . . .'

For some reason, my utterance of the phrase '*diu mian zi*' seemed to infuriate her and confirm all her misgivings. It was simply too colloquial and was a phrase she herself would have used in similar circumstances. She turned on me with a vengeance and said disdainfully, 'You are no American physician!

You are a Chinese tour guide! If you are an American, then I am an American too!'

At that moment the door flew open and Bob rushed in with our friends. He placed his arm around my shoulders and explained that he had taken a wrong turn and lost his way. Even though Bob's parents were from China and his features were Chinese, the saleswoman took one look at him and said to me, 'Why didn't you tell me you were married to an American?'

Because of the diversity of each nation's history and culture, it is debatable whether there *is* any such thing as a universal code of logic. Concepts are expressed by words. If certain words are absent in a second language, the exact meaning of a particular concept expressed in the vocabulary of the first language may also be non-existent in the second, 'foreign' country and may not hold the same relevance there.

Any logical train of thought is related to the language of the thinker and his country's culture. Americans (or Chinese) often take the position that *their* logic is the only true logic, forgetting that *their* logic is based on *their* particular language and culture. There are certain fundamental differences between the English and Chinese languages that may lead to widely divergent world views (what the Germans call W*eltanschauung*).

Western thought is based on an underlying logic that assumes or denies the subject of a proposition. Westerners may propose that 'milk is white' and 'coal is not white'. The predicate in this proposition is 'whiteness', which is affirmed by the subject 'milk' but denied by the subject 'coal'. Westerners ask themselves, 'What *is* milk?' 'What *is* coal?' 'What *is* whiteness?' This type of logic is based on the 'law of identity'. Trying to answer the question 'what' leads to the concept of causality, substance identity and deductive reasoning.

Chinese logic is not based on subject–predicate relationships but on correlative duality. Neither subject nor predicate is necessary in a Chinese sentence. Instead of saying, 'Milk is white, but coal is not white,' we Chinese say, 'White milk, black coal.' On many occasions, the *subject* is omitted altogether. In Chinese, we cannot say, 'It snows.' Instead, we say, 'Drop snow.'

By dispensing with the subject, Chinese thought takes a different path. Attention is concentrated not on the nature of the 'thing in itself' (Kant's *das Ding an sich*) but on the total relational pattern of things in general.

Two words with opposite meanings are seldom placed together side by side in English. In contrast, we Chinese frequently use antonyms to represent a concept. Some common examples are:

OPPOSING WORDS	MEANING	CONCEPT REPRESENTED
jing 進 *tui* 退	advance/retreat	movement
shang 上 *xia* 下	above/below; up/down	all about, whole body
kai 開 *guan* 關	open/close	light switch*
cheng 成 *bai* 敗	success/failure	outcome, result
da 大 *xiao* 小	big/small	size
chang 長 *duan* 短	long/short	situation
duo 多 *shou* 少	much/little	how much or what
mei 買 *mei* 賣	buy/sell	business or trade
hei 黑 *bai* 白	black/white	morality

* Many Chinese say 'Open the light!' instead of 'Turn on the light!' when speaking English.

Antonyms are used frequently in daily speech. In a shoe-store, an assistant asks, 'Your foot, much/little big/small?' (What is the size of your foot?) A shopper asks the grocer, 'This apple, much/little money?' (How much is this apple?) One broker confesses to another, 'My buy/sell, no good. How is your buy/sell?' (My business is not good. How is your business?)

In all three cases, a topic is raised; it is then followed by a query or comment. This is similar in style to the road-sign SAN DIEGO FREEWAY, KEEP LEFT!, where the topic raised (San Diego freeway) is obviously greater and much more important than the comment that follows. This type of sentence structure may have given rise to the general Chinese notion that the universe is infinitely more complex than the sum of its parts and can never be totally understood.

Emphasis on word relations underscores the signs and functions of an object or an undertaking, rather than the underlying nature of the objects themselves. Western reality is based on substance and causality, whereas Chinese reality is centred on relative contrasts and relational thinking. This is evident in many areas of Chinese culture. Chinese cooks consider the taste, aroma and texture of all the ingredients that make up a dish and how they can best blend with each other. Confucius was concerned with the *will* of Heaven, not its *nature*. Confucianism is a code of ethics dealing with human relationships; while Chinese poetry, art and architecture all aspire towards balance and harmony.

We Chinese do not think of antonyms as irreconcilable contradictions but as interdependent complementary forces or two faces of the same coin. Placing them next to each other enables us to view a particular phenomenon from opposite standpoints while contemplating the *entire* concept.

'Search for the *li* (principle) hidden within the shape and form of each character,' my grandfather said. Then he added, 'Always respect the written word. Your grandmother's father was a herbalist. Many of his patients revered him so much that they used to brew his written prescriptions in the same pot with the medicinal herbs, as if his writing had healing power also.'

Besides conveying meaning, many commonly used Chinese characters are rich reservoirs of logic, principle and wisdom. Chinese words should be studied not only for their strokes and pronunciation but also for their conceptual philosophy.

One such word is *jiao* 教. It consists of two parts. The left side is the symbol *xiao* 孝 or 'filial piety'. The right side is 文, which means 'deep thinking' or 'intending'. The word *jiao* means 'religion' as well as 'to teach'.

If it is true that ideas determine how we perceive reality, then every time we see this word, we are linking the concepts of religion or education with intentions of filial piety by reason of resemblance, recognition and association. Confucian philosophy is based on family unity, parental respect and emphasis on education. All three elements are incorporated in the single word *jiao*. Indeed, ancestor-worship has been called the 'one true Chinese religion' by some writers.

There is an intimate connection between language and psychology. As discussed earlier, the type of language spoken by an individual appears to affect his mentality. Conversely, his culture and behaviour also influence the way in which he thinks and speaks. Each language apparently creates its own *Weltanschauung*.

Translations between Chinese and English need interpreters who are not only adept at both languages, but well versed in the two cultures. Even under ideal circumstances, diversity of historical background and traditional customs may hinder the accuracy of the transfer. Certain Chinese concepts are very difficult to render into English (and vice versa). A literal translation of a metaphor often makes no sense. In other cases, the intrinsic nature of a concept becomes distorted because no word can be found to convey its exact meaning. Italians call this phenomenon '*traduttore-traditore*' (translator-traitor).

One example of a word that is difficult to translate is the Chinese word for the colour 'white' (*bai* 白). Too often it is mistranslated because it carries so many connotations. To begin with, white is not considered a lucky colour in China. Besides being the colour of mourning and death, it also signifies uselessness and lack of success. 'White speech' 白話 means wasted argument and 'white walking' 白走 signifies effort expended in vain. 'White arrival' 白到 indicates a useless visit and 'white rice' 白飯 denotes sponging off one's host.

Two other examples of 'difficult' Chinese words are *mian zi* 面子 (face) and *guan xi* 關係 (connections).

As I mentioned earlier, *mian zi* means 'self respect or honour' and signifies a person's sense of self-worth. In China, 'face' or *mian zi* can be given, denied, begged for, borrowed, relied on, lost, sold, bought, etc. More than that, *mian zi* must be preserved, especially in front of an audience. The concept is so ingrained that it is always advisable to carry out delicate negotiations with any Chinese in private so as not to jeopardise his *mian zi*. In order to please the Chinese, try to give *mian zi* at every opportunity. It costs nothing and generates tremendous good will.

Differences between the intrinsic nature of the English and Chinese *Weltanschauung* may be observed from this true story.

Sixty-two-year-old Mrs Wang flew from Hong Kong to London to celebrate the engagement of her daughter Helen to Andrew Sutherland. Andrew was the oldest son of a prominent English banking family. At the glittering affair, all eyes were riveted on Andrew's regal mother when she walked in wearing her priceless family jewels, including a sparkling tiara resplendent with diamonds, rubies and emeralds. Helen introduced the two mothers-in-law to be, confiding to Mrs Wang that Lady Sutherland was an heiress. At the dinner table Mrs Wang complimented Lady Sutherland on her beautiful gems. She thought she was giving Lady Sutherland *mian zi* (face) as well as an opportunity to show off her wealth. The crunch came when Mrs Wang pointed to the tiara, a family heirloom, and asked loudly, 'How much that cost?'

As Helen summed up later, 'In my mother's mind, she was giving her *qin qi* 親戚 (close relative) a big dose of *mian zi*. But to Lady Sutherland, Mother's bold question was merely a vulgar invasion of her privacy.'

The Chinese term *guan xi* 關係 means relationship, connections or ties. This is the key to every transaction in China, where having a relationship is of paramount importance in getting things done. *Guan xi* expresses the same sentiment as the English saying, 'It's not *what* you know; it's *who* you know.'

An additional meaning for *guan xi* is 'to matter'. If you say in Chinese that something 'has no *guan xi*', it means that 'it doesn't matter'. The implication is that if one has no *guan xi* with a certain person, organisation or enterprise, then that party does not matter and merits no concern at all.

*

Conversely, some English words denoting common western concepts are absent in Chinese. Two examples are 'rights' and 'privacy'.

In the dictionary, 'rights' is translated as *quan* 權 (pronounced *chuan*). Human rights are called *jen quan*. *Jen* 人 means 'man'; and *quan* 權 means 'power'. But 'power' is not synonymous with 'rights'. 'Power' means the ability and authority to act, whereas a 'right' is a claim to anything that belongs to a person by law, nature or tradition. Since China has never had a traditional system of basic law, the concept of individual human rights is simply non-existent.

The Declaration of the Rights of Man was first adopted by the French during the revolution of 1789. At that time, China was still being governed by the Qing dynasty emperor Qian Long. Throughout China's long history, power (*quan*) has traditionally rested in the hands of the emperor and his officials. Government was by the rule of man, not by the rule of law. After the Qing dynasty was toppled in 1911, the baton of power was seized from the warlords by Chiang Kai-shek, then wrested from him by Mao Zedong in 1949. When Mao died in 1976 the baton passed first to Deng Xiaoping and then to Jiang Zemin after Deng's death.

Ordinary Chinese people (*lao bai xing* 老百姓 – 'old hundred names') have always been completely without *quan*. As a Shanghai cab-driver said to me, 'Whatever they like to call themselves, emperor, president or chairman, they are all the same. They and their henchmen have *quan* and I have none. So they give the orders and I obey. Everything else is foreign propaganda.'

Whenever a Chinese person reads or hears the term *quan*, he is reading or hearing the term 'power'. To the Chinese mind, the concepts of 'power' and 'rights' are so intertwined that only those who hold power have rights. No power, no rights.

For the term 'human rights' (*jen quan*) to mean what it means in the west, China first has to adopt a set of laws that will be sovereign to the power of the ruling party. This may pose difficulties. In the west there has been a long-standing conviction that 'Laws make the King; the King does not make the laws'. The western Christian belief in an almighty God has traditionally, by serendipity, subsumed political power under a higher framework of reference. There is no such precedence in China to provide for the sovereignty of a rule-based legal system.

Another problematic English word is 'privacy'. In the dictionary, 'privacy' is translated as *si* 私. But the Chinese word *si* means 'personal', 'secret', 'selfish', 'an illicit relationship', or 'ownership'. None of these corresponds exactly to 'privacy', which is a 'state of withdrawal from company' or a 'secluded retreat'.

In most Chinese families the concept of 'privacy' is absent. Homes are crowded places and few have the opportunity to either sleep in a private room or withdraw from family activity. The emphasis is not on individual wishes but on a person's relationships and moral obligations towards other members of the family.

For 155 years, between 1842 and 1997, Hong Kong was a British colony. Under British rule, many English words such as 'taxi', 'bus' and 'salad' were given a Cantonese pronunciation and incorporated wholesale into the local Cantonese dialect. As mainland China opens her doors ever wider to the west, increased trade will bring new ideas as well as goods both into and out of this populous country. What the effect on her language will be is difficult to predict, but one thing is certain. Just as Buddhism from India was mingled with Taoism and Confucianism into Zen Buddhism, so more and more western words will be fused with traditional Chinese phrases into a brave new vocabulary.

10

The Sight Strikes a Chord in my Heart

觸景生情

CHU JING SHENG QING

Feng 風 means 'wind'; *shui* 水 means 'water': *feng shui*, or 'wind and water', is a traditional Chinese concept linking the destiny of man to his environment; it aims to ensure that people live in harmony with their surroundings. Metaphorically, *feng shui* should be translated as 'geomantic omen', meaning that a person's surroundings will influence his fate. The closest equivalent to *feng shui* in the western world is astrology. *Feng shui* is an expanded Chinese version of astrology which takes into account portents inherent in earthly structures as well as in heavenly bodies that influence the future. Though it incorporates common-sense ideas such as avoiding northerly winds, floods, earthquakes and landslides, it is mainly a personal doctrine of predictions which vary according to an individual's date and time of birth, rather like the postulates of the signs of the zodiac. Sites which are propitious for one may be harmful to another. Since earthly edifices, unlike stars, can be modified and rearranged by architects, engineers, gardeners and decorators, *feng shui* aims to lay out cities, tombs, houses, offices, gardens and furniture along principles that will facilitate the flow of *qi* and promote good luck. Thus, *feng shui* adherents believe that fortune may be generated and adversity diverted simply by altering the landscape around a house or rearranging the furniture in a room.

Both wind and water convey a sense of invisible energy which flows in certain directions. As mentioned earlier, the Chinese believe in another source of energy, *qi*, which emanates from the earth's surface and can influence man's fate. This hidden force permeates the land and may be divided into *sha* 殺 (negative) *qi* or *yun* 運氣 (positive) *qi*. For some unknown reason, the word *sha*, which means 'to kill, reduce, or abate', is often used alone (in English usage) to denote malevolent *qi* or 'bad luck', whereas the word *yun*, which means 'to carry', or 'luck', is usually omitted to indicate beneficial *qi* or 'good fortune'. According to *feng shui* theories, *sha* strikes venomously from sharp edges in straight lines, whereas *qi* roams slowly along curved paths.

To the Chinese mind, the landscape is alive. Ridges on hills are seen as tigers' manes or dragons' backs and *feng shui* masters search for them in every natural vista. An ideal site would be bounded by the Green Dragon of the East, the White Tiger of the West, the Red Bird of the South and the Black Tortoise of the North. In the countryside these animals are 'discovered' in the contours of surrounding slopes, peaks and valleys; in the city, they are detected in the shapes and forms of neighbouring buildings. In modern terms, one's dream house (or tomb) should face south; on its east side there should be undulating inclines or a hill, representing the dragon; its west side should border a long, meandering path, symbolising the tiger; in front there should be the ocean or a lake, depicting the bird; behind

184

and to the north is a mountain, which represents the tortoise. The Chinese believe that death and misfortune will result if a tiger (new house to the west) is built higher than the dragon (existing house immediately to the east). If the new residence happens to belong to a westerner and the existing one to a Chinese *feng shui* believer, the resulting conflict of cultural values will probably lead to irreconcilable differences imposs-ible to resolve.

The principles of *feng shui* have been so entrenched in Chinese thought that property owners in imperial China used to possess the 'right of appeal to stop construction' if they could prove to the magistrates that their neighbour's new abode would destroy the *qi* of their own family home. (Substitute 'ocean view' for *qi* and all this will be perfectly understandable to everyone.)

There are numerous historical accounts of the influence of *feng shui* on the thought processes of Chinese officials and citizens alike. For instance, the word Kowloon (Hong Kong's mainland peninsula across the harbour) means 'nine dragons'. The city of Kowloon is said to stand on eight hills (dragons), while the ninth hill used to symbolise the emperor. A few decades after Hong Kong was ceded to the British after the Opium War of 1842, the British proposed that a telegraph line be erected between Kowloon and Canton to facilitate communication. This was bitterly opposed by Chinese *feng shui* experts, who argued that since Canton was the capital city of Guang Dong province, it was the City of Rams. Its entrance was most aus-piciously guarded by the nine dragons of Kowloon on one side and embraced by the tiger's mouth on the other. To pass a rope (telegraph line) from Hong Kong to the ram (Canton) and link the latter to barbarian company would be most foolish and dangerous, like leading lambs to the slaughter-house. The British, of course, were completely nonplussed and mystified by this line of argument. After some delay, the project was pushed through. The Chinese felt they had been coerced even though both sides eventually benefited greatly from the enterprise.

During the building of Wong Nai Chong Gap Road on Hong Kong island, the locals were upset because the British Public Works Department had 'disjointed the spine' of one of the island's main 'dragons' by insisting on pushing the road through Wong Nai Chong Gap itself. As workers dug deeper into the ground, they found that the subsoil contained clay with a high level of iron oxide, which was of a reddish-brown colour. On seeing this, *feng shui* believers immediately claimed that the diggers had caused the dragon's severed spine to bleed and that its life was in jeopardy. A memorial stone known as Jue Duan Long (Severed and Broken Dragon) was erected to commemorate the injured dragon. Those who prayed to the monument were said to have had their wishes granted.

On occasional Sunday afternoons in the 1950s, when I attended the Sacred Heart convent school, the Italian sisters used to take all the boarders to ride the Peak Tram to the top of Victoria Peak. The terminal was only a short walk from our school and this ride continues to be one of the most popular tourist attractions in Hong Kong today. At the top of Victoria Peak a circular path called Lugard Path has been engineered around the summit. I still feel a thrill whenever I retrace the walks I used to take as a schoolgirl so many years ago, and gaze down at the spectacular views from almost every angle. The Chinese name for Victoria Peak was Tai Ping Shan 太平山 (Hill of Peace), but the locals nicknamed it Lau Shou Xin 老壽星 (Old Man Star of Longevity). When the British were constructing Lugard Path, the Chinese believed that a noose was being placed around the neck of the Old Man Star of Longevity. The foreigners were violating *feng shui* principles and their rule would not last much longer. As the years went by, *feng shui* masters explained that the halter had been placed too low; this meant that death by strangulation would come about very slowly. According to them, this finally happened in 1997.

Visitors to Hong Kong are often impressed by the spectacular skyline of this futuristic city. Among the forest of skyscrapers dotting the island's Central business district are two buildings which stand out conspicuously like 'cranes in the midst of a gaggle of chickens' (*he li ji qun* 鶴立雞群). The first is the British-owned Hong Kong and Shanghai Bank, designed by Norman Foster. It is a giant post-modern steel structure constructed under the guidance of well-paid *feng shui* masters, taking into account every conceivable astrological, directional, schematic and calendrical calculation. The second is the soaring and dramatic Bank of China building, which appears to personify the essence of post-modernism. Owned by the People's Republic of China (where *feng shui* was suppressed as superstition) and designed by the noted Chinese-American architect I. M. Pei, it is through no accident the tallest high-rise in the city. Majestic, stately, imposing and aggressive, with its sharp, angular walls radiating *sha* on to its neighbours (among which is the former British governor's mansion), its very presence seems to shout to the world that China is now a country to be reckoned with.

*

Experts used to consider the *feng shui* at Hong Kong's Government House, the British governor's home, excellent. It sits at the north side of the island and is sheltered by a mountain as well as trees planted on the undulating slopes of the Botanical Garden. The harbour lies below. In addition, it is bordered by meandering roads guarding it from harmful *sha*, which can only travel in straight lines. Ever since the end of the Second World War, however, the growth and development of that particular location (known as Central), with the mushrooming of its many high-rises, has transformed its *feng shui* drastically. The erection of Hong Kong's tallest building, the Bank of China, was merely the final blow. Some in Hong Kong whisper among themselves that Britain's handover of the colony was a consequence of the *sha* from that giant bank's knife-like edges directed at Government House.

After the departure of Hong Kong's last British governor, Chris Patten, C. H. Tung was elected chief executive of the former British colony. For reasons that were never fully explained, Mr Tung refused to move into Government House and insisted on staying in his rather modest apartment, situated a safe distance away from the Bank of China. Today, Government House remains unoccupied.

On my frequent visits back to Hong Kong, I always make a point of driving by Government House, which is fronted by an impressive gate and large expanses of bright green lawn. It looks very English and rather quaint under the giant shadows of towering glass-and-steel skyscrapers all around. Not infrequently I have caught sight of tourists snapping pictures or chatting

188

amiably with the two uniformed Chinese guards at the entrance. When I was a girl, I used to be marched past this very mansion with my fellow-boarders on our way to and from Sunday mass at the Catholic cathedral. In those days the sentinels were always tall, erect, remote, English, silent and somewhat intimidating, standing at attention with their fearsome weapons and always looking straight ahead. We would hurry by with averted eyes, not daring to cast a second glance. None of us ever dared address a single remark to them. The very idea seemed preposterous. And yet, looking back, I ask myself, Why didn't we? Was it because we felt ill at ease and resentful marching by our colonial master's home? Taking our horoscopes into account, was the *feng shui* of Government House inauspicious for all Chinese schoolgirls in those days?

The rudiments of *feng shui* began in ancient China with the traditional Chinese concepts of *qi* and *yin* and *yang*. A tomb or house laid out according to the principles of *feng shui* was said to represent the visible outward signs of harmonising celestial *yin* and *yang* with the cosmic breath of *qi*. Within the house, *feng* shui declared that the rooms should be laid out according to the eight trigrams of the *I Ching* and the owner's horoscope. The five elements of wood, fire, earth, metal and water also came into play as well as certain lucky (and unlucky) numbers.

Over the centuries, these principles evolved into a complex blend of aesthetics, common sense, philosophy, mysticism and superstition. *Feng shui* plays a large part in the rites of ancestor-worship, particularly in the selection of a burial site for a parent. Besides taking into account the location of the tomb and heavenly bodies above, the time and date of burial must agree with the horoscopes of the living as well as the dead in order to bring good fortune to the entire family. Indeed, so many considerations had to be taken into account that funerals were often delayed for months, if not years. Meanwhile, the unburied body was usually kept in a coffin in the living room of the eldest son. Frequently it became a serious health hazard. The practice was so prevalent that during the Ming dynasty (1368–1644) a law was passed which decreed that the deceased had to be buried within a year. The punishment for disobedience was eighty blows with a stick.

Feng shui came to play such an important part in the selection of an ancestor's tomb because of the Chinese belief that the soul of the deceased lives on in the grave and will only respond to the entreaties of its descendants if it is completely satisfied and contented.

When my father was young, one of his high-school classmates was employed by a large, publicly traded French company. This young man used to pay his respects at his Chinese parents' grave during *qing ming* 清明 (a day in early April for remembering one's ancestors and sweeping their graves). Besides petitioning his dead ancestors, he would also 'pray' at the mausoleum of his dead French employer, whose soul, he hoped, would put in a good word (presumably in French) with the Parisian manager who had taken his place. As he told my father, 'A word from my dead French *taipan* is worth more than ten thousand words from anyone Chinese, alive or dead. Now I'm sure to get my raise.'

According to *feng shui,* numbers are also harbingers of good or bad luck. The number 13 is considered lucky in China, being the number of months in a lunar year. So are the numbers 8, 9, 5 and 6. In Cantonese 8 sounds like another word 發, which means 'rising development'; the number 88 resembles the Chinese character for double happiness 囍. 9 is pronounced *jiu,* which is also the pronunciation of a word 久 that means 'a long, long time' or 'never changing'; hence it signifies longevity. 5 is the number of Chinese elements and is considered lucky as it represents the five elements of wood, fire, earth, metal and water. The number 6 has the same pronunciation in Cantonese as the character 祿, which means 'salary' and therefore signifies wealth.

Number 4 is an unlucky number because it sounds like the word *si* 死, which means 'death' in both Mandarin and Cantonese. The number 1 is also unpopular because the Chinese character for 1 (*yi* —) resembles a bar across a closed door, like a prison gate.

There is so much demand for lucky numbers that wealthy Chinese often spend unbelievable sums to purchase certain popular numbers such as 8888 for automobile licence plates and telephones, etc. The Hong Kong government holds periodic auctions where desirable numbers are sold and bidding is fast and furious. Personal numbers which have a special meaning (such as birthdates and anniversaries) are also sought after and considered lucky.

Feng shui appears to be gaining popularity in the west. Newspapers in some major American cities (such as the *Los Angeles Times*) even have regular question and answer columns on *feng shui.* In April 2000 it was reported in the London *Times* that the British Tomato Growers' Association were planning to use *feng shui* to boost the production of their tomato crop! Because dates play such an important part in *feng shui*, it is essential to get them right. My grandfather once related this fascinating true story about the Chinese calendar.

'Only the emperor and his appointed Bureau of Astronomy were permitted to study the stars and compile the imperial calendar. Others were prohibited from carrying out this work. The calendar was a document of the highest importance because, as son of Heaven, the emperor had to ensure that there was harmony between Heaven, earth and man. Each copy was wrapped in imperial yellow silk and distributed personally by the emperor to his chief ministers, who received it on their knees. It was then dispatched throughout the empire.

'By the fourteenth century BC we Chinese had already established the solar year at 365¼ days and the lunar month at 29½ days. Each month begins with the day of a new moon and has either 29 days or 30 days. In order to reconcile the annual difference of 11¼ days between the solar and lunar systems (365¼-354), an extra month called an "intercalary month" or "leap month" was added every two to three years. When I was a boy, the emperor himself decided when the day of each new year should begin or whether an extra month should be added to that particular year. Since our Chinese calendar took into account the sun as well as the moon, we called it Yin-Yang Li 陰/陽歷 or lunar-solar calendar.

'An accurate calendar was essential to the practice of *feng shui* because of the belief that the movement of the stars had an influence on human destiny. The fortune of every marriage,

192

burial, birth, business transaction, journey, or any other conceivable activity, depended on it falling on a "suitable" day, as calculated by the *feng shui* masters, who consulted the calendar. An error in the imperial calendar would mean that all the days of that year would be wrong and that *feng shui* predictions would be meaningless and the whole exercise fraudulent.

'The understanding of astronomy is intimately linked to the knowledge of mathematics. Without mathematics, astronomy cannot advance. Before the Yuan dynasty (1279–1368), Chinese astronomy used to be superior to that of other nations. After the Arabs and Europeans adopted the symbol zero and the Hindu-Arabic numeral system, they made dramatic strides in their knowledge of mathematics (and astronomy) and soon surpassed us. The Mongol Kublai Khan, who conquered China in 1279, started the tradition of employing Muhammadan scholars with mathematical training from Arab sources to run the Bureau of Astronomy and compile the calendar.

'When the Italian Jesuit priest Matteo Ricci (1552–1610) came to China, the Gregorian calendar had just been drawn up in Rome by the great Jesuit mathematician Christopher Clavius, who happened to be Ricci's teacher. Clavius himself was a friend of Kepler and Galileo. Ricci took the new calendar with him to China in 1582, the same year that it was first used by the Europeans. During his twenty-eight years in China Ricci greatly impressed the scholar-mandarins with his learning. His astronomical calculations were acknowledged to be more accurate than those of either the Chinese or the Muhammadan astronomers and he was asked to help the government with his observations of the stars.

'After Ricci's death his successors Adam Schall von Bell and Ferdinand Verbiest were given the prestigious posts of assistant

193

directors in the Imperial Bureau of Astronomy to help reform the Chinese calendar. This caused jealousy between various rival astronomical groups. The displaced Chinese head of the bureau, Yang Kuang Hsien, became increasingly bitter. Two contests were held between Chinese, Jesuit and Muhammadan astronomers to predict eclipses. Despite the fact that they won the contests, the Jesuits were convicted of high treason and condemned to die after bribes amounting to 400,000 taels of silver were paid by Yang to those in power. While they awaited execution, a terrible earthquake shook the city of Beijing and 300,000 people perished. The palace caught fire and a dust storm darkened the sky. These were considered to be such powerful omens that the regents released the Jesuits – unfortunately the elderly, frail and paralysed Schall died three months later in 1666.

'Verbiest was reinstated at the Bureau of Astronomy when the young emperor Kang Hsi took over control of the government in 1671. Verbiest had won yet another contest against Yang Kuang Hsien by correctly calculating where the shadow of a sundial would fall at noon the next day. Yang, who was ignorant of mathematics and could not make the calculation, was dismissed from his post and banished to Tartary. Verbiest was also instrumental in correcting the Chinese calendar by removing an intercalary month that had been erroneously inserted two years earlier in 1669. Even today, the date of the Chinese New Year is still calculated according to the methods set down by Schall and Verbiest.

'After China became a republic in 1911, we finally adopted the Gregorian calendar in place of our Yin-Yang Li.* However,

* For an explanation of the various calendrical systems, see the Note at the end of this chapter, page 205.

we did not abandon the Yin-Yang Li and kept it as well. Thus Chinese New Year can fall anytime between late January and the middle of February on the Gregorian calendar.

'Unlike the Gregorian calendar, where years are dated in a linear fashion from the birth of Jesus Christ, our Chinese calendar is cyclical and is repeated every twelve years. We have named one of twelve animals as a symbol for each year and the same animal returns every twelve years. The year 2000 means 2000 years after the birth of Christ in the Gregorian calendar but it will be the year of the dragon in the Chinese calendar.

'Legend has it that many years ago all the animals were invited to come and visit Buddha but only twelve showed up. They came in the following order: rat, ox, tiger, rabbit, dragon, snake, horse, sheep, monkey, rooster, dog and pig. Buddha named a year after each animal as they appeared. Now I was born in 1878, which was the year of the tiger. Since the year of the tiger comes around every twelve years, people born in 1890, 1902, 1914, 1926, 1938 and 1950 were all born in the year of the tiger. Those born in 1879 were born in the year of the rabbit; whereas 1880 was the year of the dragon, and so on.'

Although much of modern *feng shui* theory probably arose from the fervid imagination of unscrupulous *feng shui* 'practitioners', there is some evidence that the belief may have originated from the ancient Chinese awareness of the earth's inherent magnetism.

Geomagnetism, also called terrestrial magnetism, is the natural magnetism of the earth – the invisible and somewhat mysterious force which directs the compass needle north/

south and is also capable of bending light waves as well as radio waves. Since ancient times, the Chinese have seen the earth's magnetic field as something magical and awesome. The belief that tombs, houses and cities should be aligned harmoniously with this *'qi of the earth'* may have given rise to the concept of *feng shui* in the first place.

In the year 1086, during the Northern Song dynasty, the Chinese scientist and writer Shen Kua 沈括 wrote in his book *Dream Pool Essays*:

> Magicians rub the point of a needle with the lodestone; then it is able to point to the south. But it always inclines slightly to the east, and does not point directly at the south . . . It is best to suspend the needle by a single cocoon fibre of new silk attached to the centre of the needle with a piece of wax the size of a mustard seed – then, hanging in a windless place, it will always point to the south. Among such needles there are some which, after being rubbed, point to the north.
>
> I have needles of both kinds.

This is because the earth's true geographical north and south poles are about 1200 miles away from the magnetic north and south poles: a phenomenon known as the 'magnetic declination' of the earth's magnetic field. The angle of variation between the earth's true pole and its magnetic pole is not constant but shifts gradually. Sir William Gilbert (physician to Queen Elizabeth I) was the first scientist in Britain to write of this in his book *De Magnete*. However, as Shen Kua proved, the Chinese knew about this angle of variation hundreds of years before the west.

Some antique geomancers' compasses manufactured in China hundreds of years ago have two different sets of compass points among the many concentric circles around the pointer. These compass points show the magnetic declination at two different times in the past. They are a few degrees apart from each other, thus illustrating our forefathers' awareness of the shift in magnetic declination during two distinct and separate historical eras.

The Chinese were also aware, long before the rest of the world, of another characteristic that is peculiar to magnets. Magnetism is not retained for ever but can be destroyed by heat. If a magnet is heated above a temperature known as the Curie point (which varies according to the metal), it loses its magnetism.

Conversely, if a piece of metal is heated to a high temperature, and subjected to a magnetic field by being placed next to a lodestone, it will take on the magnetic properties of the lodestone as it cools down to (and below) its Curie point. This is called 'magnetic remanence' and induction. Since the earth has a weak magnetic field of its own, known as the geomagnetic field, a piece of red-hot metal will acquire the earth's magnetism if it is aligned carefully in the north–south direction as it cools through its Curie point.

The Chinese knew of the induction of remanent magnetism by the earth's geomagnetic field and its importance in battle. In the year 1044 Tseng Dung-liang wrote:

> When soldiers lose their way during bad weather or black nights, and they know not where to go, they either let an old horse lead them, or use the south-pointing fish to find their direction. They cut a thin sheet of iron into the shape of a fish about two inches long and half an inch wide, with a pointed head and tail. They then heat this in a fire, and when it is thoroughly heated, they use iron tongs to place it with its tail pointing north. They then quench it with water in a basin, and keep it in a closed box with a tight lid. To use it, they fill a small bowl with water in a windless place, and lay the fish flat upon

the surface of the water so that it floats, whereupon its head will point south.

Joseph Needham, author of *Science and Civilization in China*, thought that the 'tightly closed box' mentioned above probably contained a lodestone base to 'nourish and strengthen' the iron fish, which had been magnetised through thermoremanence. The Chinese obviously considered the earth's magnetic field to be a living and active force, able to impart its magic to other metals. In 1609, during the late Ming dynasty, Wang Chi described the lodestone in his book *Universal Encyclopaedia* almost as if it were supernatural:

> The *qi* of the lodestone is as if it were alive. It has a head and a tail. Its head points north and its tail south. The force of the head is stronger than that of the tail. If it is broken, all the smaller pieces also have heads and tails. If it's heated in the fire, it 'dies' and is no longer able to point.

The oldest compass discovered in China was used not for navigational, but for *feng shui* geomantic purposes. Known also as a *luo pan* 羅盤 (reticulated disc), the geomantic compass had a pointer, which used to be made of lodestone in the shape of a spoon with its handle pointing south. The *luo pan*s that are used today consist of a wooden disc, painted yellow, about ten inches in diameter, with a small, steel needle at the centre pointing north. (According to Joseph Needham, the needle replaced the spoon as a pointer in China in the seventh or eighth century AD.) Radiating from the middle are concentric rings containing information on planetary movements; magnetic correlations; *yin* and *yang*; *pa gua* 陰陽八卦 (eight trigrams from the *I Ching*); the twelve animals of the Chinese zodiac; the five elements; the four seasons; the Chinese calendar, etc.

Geomantic compasses vary in design. Some contain up to forty concentric circles of information, each with different numbers measuring various phenomena according to Chinese beliefs. Others contain less than ten circles. By reading off the numbers on the compass, *feng shui* practitioners attempt to harmonise and align different forces of nature at any particular location with a client's date, year and time of birth. Much depends on a practitioner's interpretation and ingenuity.

What do I think of all this? I'll summarise my feelings by telling you of a Chinese-American restaurant within walking distance of our house that advertises:

CANTONESE, SZECHWAN, HUNAN AND SHANGHAI CUISINE
also
VIETNAMESE, CAMBODIAN, KOREAN AND THAI DISHES
besides
STEAK, LOBSTER, FRENCH FRIES, REFRIED BEANS!

This menu evokes in me the same emotional response as the geomantic compass. It's as if they're both terrified of leaving anything out. JUST IN CASE! The result is a chop suey of every idea (or recipe) under the sun and a suspicion that they may not be proficient in any.

Over the centuries, the theories of *feng shui* were applied to everything from the selection of tombs to the planning of entire cities, from the orientation of palaces to the arrangement of flowers. Outside China, its influence can be seen today in many Asian countries such as Burma, Vietnam, Singapore, Malaysia, Korea and Japan.

There is no doubt that a harmonious and pleasing environment encourages serenity and happiness. *Feng shui* masters have blended our desire for harmony, beauty and good luck into an art that is part architectural design, part interior decoration and part superstition.

According to *feng shui* theories, outside the house, one should avoid having mounds, boulders or trees blocking the entrance. The front door must not open on to a sharp bend in a river or a straight road; otherwise secret arrows of *sha* will be able to shoot straight into the house. Where this is unavoidable, the door should be set at an angle. Curved paths and meandering streams leading to the entrance are most propitious because beneficial *qi* moves gently along these lines. Avoid buying a house facing angular roof lines, sharp corners and tall poles which can shoot 'poison arrows' into the property. A talisman considered very powerful and often hung outside the house to dispel any such *sha* is a *pa kua* mirror. This is a convex mirror with the eight trigrams of the *I Ching* painted in gold on a red frame. The Chinese believe that mirrors deflect the path of evil spirits because these can only travel forwards in a straight line; the mirrors force them to turn back to their source.

If you go for a walk through some of Hong Kong's residential areas, you may notice these mirrors placed at odd angles at some corner houses and business establishments, especially if they face a road which leads directly into the building. Some of the mirrors may be reinforced with the *pa gua* 八卦 (eight trigrams) to ward off the *sha* of evil spirits. Occasionally, 'counter' mirrors on neighbouring houses are positioned to send back the rays from the first set of mirrors.

The ideal site for a building is square or rectangular because these shapes represent earth and therefore stability. Triangular and odd-shaped lots are undesirable because they symbolise fire and danger. Sharp corners and square pillars within a building are to be avoided because they give rise to inauspicious arrows of *sha* internally. The dramatic lobby of the Grand Hyatt Hotel in Hong Kong is supported by huge, spectacular cylindrical columns of black granite erected at vast expense. Mirrors are used to give an illusion of space inside a small room but are never placed to reflect the door. Otherwise, beneficial *qi* would be deflected out of the room as soon as the door was opened.

The front door must not lead directly on to a stairway or face a mirror but open inwards into a bright foyer. This allows *qi* to enter the house and bring good luck to the residents. In the living room fireplaces, plants, aquariums and decorative waterfalls are best sited on the south or south-east side, easily located with the help of a compass. Supposedly, this is the corner where beneficial *qi* is generated and stored. Both water and fire energise the rest of the house and are thought to bring prosperity.

My grandfather's bedroom in Hong Kong was small and narrow. Although his eyesight was poor, he placed his bed against the wall rather than by the window, where daylight could fall on his book. In addition, he kept a screen in front of his bedroom door, which impeded access. I once questioned him about his furniture arrangement. 'When we first moved into this flat,' he told me, 'your father's landlord, who is a *feng shui* expert, recommended that we arrange the furniture this way. He said that *feng* (wind) symbolises "direction" and *shui* (water) represents "wealth". He advised your father to buy this screen and place it at this spot because my bed must never face the door or be placed next to the window. This screen serves the dual purpose of preventing my soul from leaving my body in a premature death and of channelling beneficial *qi* to circulate gently around the screen into my room.'

I must have looked dubious because he added, 'I'm not asking you to believe this. *Feng shui* is a mixture of common sense and superstition. Our landlord is persuasive and has become very rich from his practice. We are all searching for good luck and *feng shui* masters cater to this desire. It is imposs-ible to prove or disprove what they say because they always have an explanation which sounds plausible. In any case, this screen is your father's way of demonstrating his filial piety because he took a lot of trouble over its purchase. Every time I see it, it reminds me of his affection. *Chu jing sheng qing* 觸景生情 (The sight strikes a chord in my heart). Besides, when the weather is hot, I can leave my door open and still not be seen by the servants.'

Three years later my parents moved from this small Kowloon apartment into a large house on Stubbs Road, which they rented with an option to buy. The house was said to have the best *feng shui* in Hong Kong, with the mountain behind and harbour in front, knolls to the left and rocks to the right of the entrance (representing the dragon and tiger), and a winding path skirting the front gate instead of a straight road.

Three months after moving in, my grandfather died. My father was unhappy but the *feng shui* master explained that Ye Ye was in poor health and, at seventy-four, could not be expected to live for ever. Besides, Father's businesses were pros-pering to such an extent that he was becoming known as one of Hong Kong's richest men. His four sons were all in good health. (His three daughters were not mentioned because they simply didn't count.)

Father was mollified but not entirely convinced. To hedge his bets, he continued to rent but did not exercise his option to purchase.

Another year went by. Then disaster struck. In 1953 my thirteen-year-old half-brother Franklin came down with polio after eating unwashed strawberries and died at Queen Mary's Hospital. He was the only son of my father and stepmother and, as such, was their heir-apparent as well as their favourite. This time, the *feng shui* masters could not give an adequate explanation to satisfy them. Nobody could.

Blaming Franklin's demise on bad *feng shui*, my father and Niang moved out of the Stubbs Road house, but never got over Franklin's death; and they mourned him for the rest of their lives.

For me personally, apart from the death of my grandfather, 1952 was a very auspicious year, for it was then that I won the international play-writing competition, which changed my life for ever. Somehow, my unexpected victory seemed to convince my father that I was worthy to be sent to medical school in England. Perhaps my parents' *feng shui* did not affect me because I was allowed to live in that house for only two weeks before I left for Oxford.

My opinion is that other than the usual, common sense, aesthetic aspects of *feng shui*, linking 'destiny with location' appears to be based mostly on superstition, as illustrated by the following incident, which I encountered in California in 1976.

After the birth of our daughter Ann we were in need of a bigger place and made a down payment on the house of our dreams. In order to complete the transaction, we needed to sell our old residence. To our delight, the very first couple who came to view our house made us a full-price offer. Mr and Mrs Jiang were young Chinese professionals from Taiwan who expressed a wish to move in as soon as possible.

Two days before the sale was supposed to go through, the Jiangs phoned and cancelled the deal. They were reluctant to give a reason. I must have sounded disappointed because a week later I received an explanation by mail:

> We truly love your house. It's in great condition. How-ever, my wife's cousin tells us that the *feng shui* is terrible. As a Chinese, you must understand that we cannot ignore this. The entrance to your home leads directly onto a major road. This is unacceptable because money will drain away and secret arrows of *sha* will be directed inward at us constantly. Therefore, even though your house is very fairly priced, we have decided not to buy it.

We borrowed some funds from the bank and, after a delay of three months, were able to sell our house at a much higher price. At the close of the transaction I telephoned the Jiangs, informed them of the sale, and asked whether they had pur-chased another house.

'I'm afraid not,' Mr Jiang answered after a pause. 'When we walked away from buying your house, we had $30,000 in the bank and nowhere to spend it. Somehow or other, my wife's cousin convinced us to invest the whole sum in a car wash business he was starting. I'm afraid his venture is losing money week after week and we'll probably end up with no house and no cash. I should never have believed his *feng shui* theories.'

So, for me, the rules of *feng shui* are not commandments, although an awareness of the location of our dwellings (and graves) does imbue us with a reverence for the power, harmony and beauty of our surroundings. We have all walked into places where we felt instantly comfortable and at home. *Feng shui* is an art of placement, allocating site, view, light, shapes, sizes, colours, plants and furniture to create a balanced environment. I doubt very much that hanging a mirror outside the front door or changing a stairway will alter a person's ultimate destiny. However, there is no doubt that for the majority of people, bright, tidy, spacious, cheerful rooms are more conducive to happiness and creativity than cluttered, dark, dingy, chaotic ones. Thus *feng shui* is important for its ability to provide a continuous thread of cognisance that binds us to the heavens above and the earth below, and helps us to balance our surroundings in such a way as will bring us health, wealth, happiness and the time to enjoy them all.

A Note on Calendars

There are two types of calendar: lunar and solar. Most countries started off with the lunar calendar but the Egyptians adopted the solar calendar 6000 years ago.

The moon takes 29½ days to circle around the earth. This is known as a month. There are twelve months per year and the lunar year has 354 days.

The earth takes 365.242199 days – or 365 days, 5 hours,

48 minutes and 45.96768 seconds – to circle around the sun every year.

In order to correlate the lunar year with the solar year, intercalary (leap) months or days have to be added from time to time, approximately eleven days per year.

In 45 BC Julius Caesar consulted the Greek astronomer Sosigenes to compile the Roman calendar. Sosigenes recommended that Caesar should adopt the Egyptian solar calendar of 365¼ days per year by having 365 days every year and inserting an extra 'leap day' of 366 days every four years. This Julian calendar was used until 1582.

However, by rounding off the year at 365.25 instead of 365.242199 days, 'Julian time' was being measured by a 'clock' that was running a few minutes too fast annually. Consequently, every year fell short by 11 minutes and 14.033232 seconds. As the centuries rolled by, the Julian calendar was gaining time and accumulating extra days at the rate of seven days every thousand years. The vernal equinox that was supposed to fall on 21 March was actually falling on 28 March by the year AD 1000.

In 1578 Pope Gregory XIII appointed the great mathematician Christopher Clavius to reform the calendar. A papal bull was issued in 1582 and the following measures were adopted:

- Ten days were taken off the calendar. Thus 4 October 1582 became 15 October 1582.
- Each year was given 365.2422 days instead of 365.25 days.
- Because the Julian calendar had been given too many leap years, after 1582 those leap years that fall at the turn of a century are no longer given an extra day. Thus, the year 1900 had only 365 days.
- To make the calculations even more accurate, those

century years that are divisible by four are given an extra day. Thus the year 2000 was a leap year, with 366 days. This type of leap year occurs once every 400 years.

The Gregorian calendar now differs from the solar year by only 25.96 seconds per year, or approximately by one day every 2800 years.

11

Frog at the Bottom of a Well

井底之蛙

JING DI ZHI WA

Zhuang Zi, the founder of Taoism, told the story of a frog who lived at the bottom of a well.

One day Frog saw a turtle looking down at him.

'Turtle,' Frog said, 'you have no idea what a great place I live in. When I'm restless, I hop along its coping. When tired, I rest at a crevice along its wall. When hot, I swim in its water or play in its shade. Why don't you come down and see for yourself how wonderful it is?'

Tempted, the turtle prepared to jump. Placing his left foot in, he suddenly caught his right foot on the railing along the well's edge. He retreated and said, 'Frog, your quarters are so small I daren't go down. Why don't you come and visit my home in the ocean, instead? It's tens of thousands of miles wide and thousands of yards deep. In times of floods, its waters rise only a little. In times of drought, its waters hardly fall. Surely, that's more interesting than your well?'

On hearing this, the frog became silent and could only stare at the turtle in amazement.

The moral of this story is not to have a limited outlook on life or a narrow view of the world.

When I was growing up with my six siblings during the 1940s and 1950s, our childhood home was a microcosm of the racist world beyond our walls. My mother had died of puerperal fever two weeks after my birth. My father remarried one year later and our stepmother Niang always called herself French even though she was actually half French and half Chinese. Father, who was born in 1907 in the French Concession of Shanghai, invariably introduced Niang proudly to his friends as his French wife (*fa guo tai tai* 法國太太); never his Chinese or Eurasian wife. To the Chinese of Father's era, born in the foreign concessions of treaty ports like Shanghai or Tianjin, the lowliest French citizen was deemed better than the mightiest Chinese mandarin. When my stepmother, who was beautiful, intelligent, educated, trilingual and thirteen years younger than Father, consented to marry him, he thought himself the luckiest man in the world and was dominated by her for the rest of his life.

There were seven children in our family, five from Father's first wife (my mother) and two from our stepmother. Though we all lived under one roof in a large and luxurious house, our stepmother divided our family into two separate classes. She and my father and their two children were the upper class, whereas we five stepchildren were considered second class – because, according to our stepmother, we had inherited 'bad blood' from our own dead mother.

Our Shanghai home was a veritable police state headed by our tyrannical stepmother, whose power was absolute and whose every whim had to be obeyed. We lower-class citizens languished in segregated quarters, enduring lives marred by daily injustice and crippled by discrimination. Her reign of terror was accentuated by the usual sequels of a corrupt dictatorship: overt flattery, festering resentment, palace intrigues, secret plots, greed, lies and conspiracies. That's how we grew up.

Our inferiority was reinforced by influences from both within and without our home. Inside, the wishes and desires of Niang's two children always took precedence, even though we were so much bigger and older. Outside, our foreign rulers (Japanese, French and British) demonstrated their superiority over and over in a self-imposed artificial manner – a manner slavishly imitated and mirrored at home by our parents.

This meant that Father and Niang had to prove that they were superior to us at every instant of the day or night. Throughout the many family meals we ate together, the two of them were always perfectly dressed, with not a hair out of place. Even at the height of a Shanghai heatwave my father invariably wore a jacket and tie when he came down to dinner, the sweat pouring down his face and staining his back and armpits. Like white bosses in front of their native servants, my parents stifled any sign of tenderness, weakness or vacillation in front of us in order to maintain the appearance of authority and dignity at all times. In doing so, ironically, they condemned themselves to self-imposed discomfort for life.

We, in turn, were intimidated into a timid and wary silence. For the first fourteen years of my life I don't recall having opened my mouth once to offer a single spontaneous remark during any of the meal-times I shared with them. Day after day, I cowered at their dinner table in silent terror, feeling worthless and ugly, hoping to escape unnoticed. Whenever they spoke my name, my appetite would vanish and my mind would fill with dread.

After I graduated from medical school, I spent a year working at a hospital in Hong Kong in a vain attempt to gain my parents' approval. Every Sunday evening my brothers and I were expected to dine at our parents' flat. I came to loathe the prejudices they expressed at the table but attendance was obligatory. Though I often seethed with frustrated discontent, I never dared voice my objections because challenging them would have brought about a complete break. My father and Niang were not the sort to countenance disagreement.

I used to write my personal opinions down on paper and show them to my brother James. Invariably he would scoff at them and advise me to 'go along' with the 'Old Man' and 'Old Lady'. 'What does it matter *what* you think?' he would say. 'Agree with them and make them happy. After all, they are our bread and butter and are in total control.'

When I consulted my Aunt Baba by mail, she disagreed.

In the long run, what we think does matter [she wrote]. In fact, every idea we profess, and every action we undertake influences the formation of our own character. *Jin zhu zhe chi, jin mo zhe hei* 近朱者赤, 近墨者黑 (near vermilion, one gets stained red; near ink, one gets stained black). In the evolution of the person that becomes you, a difference of opinion with your parents should not be perceived as heresy, but as an opportunity for your own individual growth and development.

All of us are ruled by ideas. They lay the scaffolding on which we base our actions. At the end of the day, a person's character is made or unmade by the intentions behind her behaviour. If you should tolerate an evil deed by looking the other way, you have already compromised your integrity even though you may think you have remained innocent and uninvolved. Eventually, a deception that you have secretly condoned in the hidden recesses of your mind will be routinely manifested by you in public without a second thought.

Young people your age may believe that ethics are irrelevant. I have heard your older sister say that the terms 'good' and 'bad' have little meaning because nothing is absolute. According to her, morality is only a question of opinion.

It is true that evil has become so prevalent and so atrocious that our senses are numbed. When we see unwanted baby girls wrapped in newspapers abandoned on the streets we are confused as to what to do. Most people simply put on a cloak of indifference and walk by with averted eyes, because ignoring what's going on and taking no action feels more comfortable, seems the easiest way.

But there is a price attached to this neglect which will eventually be extracted. By allowing corruption we will gradually form a callus over our own conscience and come to resemble the transgressors whose crookedness we have overlooked.

Her letter continued,

Have you ever thought to yourself, What is the purpose of life? What makes me happy? Is it money? Fame? A harmonious marriage? Good friends? Longevity?

I tell you happiness is not the result of a sudden stroke of good luck such as making a big win at the *mah jong* table. Even if you did make such a win, the surge of

213

elation would probably only last for a few days but you would soon get used to your new status. And everything would gradually settle down as before.

Nor is happiness dependent on fortune, fame or longevity. The rich and famous are not necessarily happier than you or me; whereas longevity without good health is a fate worse than death.

At your age the concept of 'what makes life happy' is worth thinking about. Open your eyes and look around you. Do not be a *jing di zhi wa* 井底之蛙 (frog at the bottom of a well). When you have reached a conclusion after proper reflection, act accordingly.

Over the years I have often mulled over the contents of Aunt Baba's letter, which I received thirty-five years ago. It is as relevant today as it was then. Now that my aunt is gone and I myself am in the last third of my life, I have the following suggestions to offer.

The four most vital ingredients for happiness are: *health, congenial relationships, gainful employment* and *appreciation of life's blessings.*

Longevity without good health is not desirable. Besides following the usual maxims of maintaining ideal weight, eating properly and exercising regularly, it is important to allow oneself plenty of sleep. For some reason (especially as we get older) our sense of well-being is increasingly influenced by the quality and length of our sleep. We fall into restful sleep when our mind is tranquil and our conscience clear. It is a natural state that is within everyone's reach.

Harmonious relationships are equally important. It is essential to maintain friendships at home and at work. In the buy/sell equation that is operative between two parties, always aim to be more forgiving and generous. Permit the score to be in the other side's favour. Or at least, don't keep too close a count of what is owed. Let (讓 *ran*) your partner or friend win from time to time. He or she knows just as well as you do what the score is and will return the favour in kind in due course.

We all need a goal – an enjoyable job (or hobby) we consider useful (or challenging) that gives us satisfaction and recognition. Happiness is made up of the little triumphs and small windfalls that punctuate our daily lives. It is a good dinner shared with loved ones at home; the comfort of knowing that there is a nest-egg in the bank, earned by our own honest labour; the taste of an icy cold drink on a blazing hot afternoon after a busy day at the office; or the luxury of relaxing in a hot shower after a hard-fought tennis game.

Every day and every experience is unique but nobody is happy all the time. For a person to be able to appreciate his blessings and recognise the sensation of happiness, he unfortunately has first to undergo the experience of deprivation. Sigmund Freud once described happiness as the 'satisfaction of pent-up needs'.

Most of us go through life amassing as much money and property as we can, sometimes ignoring pleas from people close to us and turning a blind eye to requests from those in need.

My father, who was already a millionaire at the age of twenty-one, was too mean to lend me the money for an airline ticket from Hong Kong to New York when I got my first job in America. At the age of seventy he was still wearing the same suit he had worn thirty years earlier. When he died, he left a fortune of over US$30 million, but every penny had already been appropriated by my stepmother before his death.

In the twilight of his time, before Alzheimer's destroyed his mind for ever – I had the rare opportunity of speaking to him without my stepmother's presence. I asked him about his past. When was the happiest time of his life?

The happiest time of his life, so he told me in 1977 at the age of sixty-nine, was when he was a young man in Tianjin. He had started his own company and was doing well. He began to export walnuts and drove from field to field inspecting the quality of the kernels. He used to set off at dawn and soon it was dark again and time to hurry home for dinner. He would be famished and suddenly realise he had eaten nothing all day. Those years were definitely the happiest time of his life.

I pictured him young, healthy and dynamic, rushing from farm to farm in pursuit of his dream – a dream he was creating and which he perceived as being worthwhile and full of purpose: establishing relationships, generating jobs, building connections, gaining experience, exporting produce, making profits, feeling optimistic.

Since then I have asked many men and women the same question. When was the happiest time of their lives? The vast majority have given me a similar reply. It was that scintillating period when they stood at the threshold of triumph. They were still a long way from the summit but the objective was in sight.

They described their sense of joyful anticipation as they watched their project take shape. I was repeatedly told that their happiest years were spent on the 'journey' towards their goal. The striving and the expectation of achievement were consistently more exhilarating than the fulfilment of the dream itself. Some frankly admitted that reaching their destination was an anti-climax.*

My father said, 'During that period, I remember getting up in the morning simply itching to get to work. My whole being was suffused with hope. It was indescribable to see my company expanding day by day. Nothing since has matched those years of buoyant optimism. To see my own brainchild transformed into reality! To gain recognition and eminence through my own efforts. Surely that is the true spice of life against which everything else pales by comparison.'

How did that buoyant young man turn into the tight-fisted Scrooge who paid his sons barely a living wage and refused to lend his daughter the price of an airline ticket to begin a new life in America? Could he have kept his *joie de vivre* if he had been more generous and loving to those around him? Paradoxically, in my case, his denial and consistent rejection infused me with the determination to make it on my own. Would I have had the same drive if he had pampered me and

* The *Los Angeles Times* recently reported that increasing numbers of young 'dot.com' millionaires who have sold their start-up companies for enormous sums are consulting psychiatrists in the Silicon Valley complaining of 'bore-dom' and 'loss of purpose'.

given me everything I asked for during my childhood and youth, as he did for my half-brother Franklin, his son by Niang? Is giving too much to our children as harmful as giving too little?

Wealthy individuals often set up trust funds for their children and grandchildren without taking into account the effects such large sums of money might have on young lives.

I have a friend whose father left a substantial sum of money to his grandson (her son) on his twenty-first birthday. The boy, who was personable but not scholarly, soon dropped out of college and spent his days sleeping and 'enjoying' himself. When challenged, he asked his mother why he should work for $7 an hour when he already had more than he could ever spend.

'I'm afraid my father made a horrible mistake,' my friend confessed. 'Here was my bright-eyed happy boy, rushing off to his part-time job at McDonald's after classes and singing his head off, proud because the owner had singled him out for promotion as night supervisor.

'His grandfather leaves him all that money and he suddenly becomes a different person. Today I phone him at 1 p.m. and he is still in bed. I ask him why he is not in class and he says he is bored with school. He tells me he doesn't know what he wants to do with himself.

'On reflection, I think the money is destroying him. It is poisoning everything that makes life most enjoyable. It is killing my boy's motivation and ambition. He has lost his purpose entirely. Instead of doing him a favour, his grandfather has damaged him.'

If the greatest source of happiness for the majority of people is the pursuit of a goal perceived as being purposeful and useful, then the rich run the risk of eradicating their children's chief fountainhead of joy by leaving them large legacies. Money not earned is not appreciated in the same way as money earned. Inheritance money is merely another name for a handout. In addition, expectation of a large legacy has been known to destroy a child's motivation and corrupt his character. Lacking gainful employment, your heirs may spend their time plotting and scheming for a larger share of your estate. Beware of your wealth being a curse instead of a blessing to your children.

Wise billionaires such as Warren Buffet have come to the same conclusion. Mr Buffet has announced publicly that he will leave each of his children only US$1–2 million. The rest of his billions will be left to charity. Why is he not leaving his vast estate to his children? Because, when all is said and done, what *is* the measure of a life? Is it how long? Is it how much? Or is it how useful and how good?

When my father died in 1988 after suffering from Alzheimer's for eleven years, my siblings and I were summoned back to Hong Kong for the reading of his will. There, at the prestigious offices of Johnson, Stokes & Masters, we were told by our stepmother to hand back the will, still unread. She informed us that our father's will was meaningless because he had no money in his estate.

My stepmother outlived my father by only two years. She spent her widowhood in her high-rise Hong Kong apartment, chain-smoking and plotting against us, her stepchildren, as well as against her own daughter. Her will was written in such a way as to cause maximum strife and discord between my siblings and me.

Throughout my years as a physician I have treated many terminally ill patients. If they spoke to me at all during their final hours, they invariably told the truth. Not once did anyone deliberately lie to me while on their death-bed. Yet this was precisely what my stepmother did. Up until the last she wanted to make me believe that she loved me – so that the hurt would be that much greater when I finally learned the truth: that she actually hated me and had secretly robbed me of my father's legacy.

Death is not something anyone enjoys planning for. We push it to the back of our minds and refuse to deal with it. As long as we are healthy, we tell ourselves that we still have a long way to go. Many of us never discuss our financial situation with our children but shroud it in secrecy. We put off writing our wills for as long as possible because we equate it with impending doom.

When we finally decide to write our will, it is usually drawn up in the privacy of an attorney's office without consulting our children (or heirs). Many would like their children (but not the children's spouses) to be the only primary beneficiaries of their estate. In such cases, the best way to protect the inheritance is to set up a living trust, where the money is left to a daughter (or son) in trust, with her as trustee and beneficiary combined. When she dies, those assets will pass to her children directly and bypass her spouse.

I have never understood why parents do not consult their children before writing their will. Why not include them? Why must the will-writing process be cloaked in secrecy? Why should our heirs not know our intentions before our demise? Why not reveal the contents to them *before* we die? Why not let them voice their opinions? Why must will-reading be such a suspenseful, nail-biting, hurtful and shocking occasion?

A parent's will is a very powerful document. It is the last and final letter from you to your heirs to be delivered after you are gone – a balance sheet of your worst and best intentions towards each of your children; a clear and unequivocal message of love or hate which will affect them and their relationship with each other for the rest of their lives. It is important to plan carefully and ponder the consequences before putting pen to paper. Before you start, ask yourself three simple questions:

How do I wish to be remembered by my loved ones?
What is my legacy?
Has my life made a difference? To anyone?

Unlike my father, I have never believed in accumulating an enormous fortune so that on my death I can leave behind as many millions as possible to my heirs. I do believe in giving my son and daughter the best education possible, so that they will gain the knowledge that will enable them to create their own future. I also believe in treating them impartially without favouritism in life as well as in my will.

It is sad but true that inherited money often means more to the donor than to the recipient. However, in order to avoid problems between siblings after death, it is wise to treat the children equally. Regardless of how many years have passed or how old they have become, siblings revert to the hierarchy of their childhood when they come together again. Suspended quarrels and dormant disagreements re-emerge and regroup with renewed vigour. No one likes to be treated differently from her siblings by their parents, let alone be singled out for disinheritance.

Some parents leave more to their poorer children and less to their richer. This is bound to create a rift. Although it may be done not out of malice, but in an attempt to provide for the less fortunate offspring, the parents will be seen as rewarding those who failed and punishing those who succeeded.

From personal experience, I know how devastating it feels to be left out. Disinheritance is the adult-life equivalent of our childhood nightmare of abandonment by our parents. More significantly, the rejection is permanent, absolute and final. Appeal is impossible and reprieve unachievable. For most of us, the yearning for parental approval never goes away. It is a primeval and visceral longing that lingers in our psyche for as long as we live. To a son or daughter, there is nothing worse than being discriminated against by our own parents. The phrase 'It's not fair!' is a common refrain heard in every household in the world.

In 1986, two years before the death of my father, I bought an airline ticket for my sister Lydia so that she could pay me a visit in California. During the ten days she stayed at my home, we spent many hours in intimate conversation about the years we had been apart. With tears in her eyes, Lydia begged me to intervene on her behalf so that she could mend her differences with our parents, from whom she had been estranged for thirty-five years, ever since she attempted to blackmail them back in 1951. Lydia told me that she wanted to see Father one last time and be a companion to Niang in her old age.

During that time Lydia would often praise me and call me *lao shi* 老實. I did not know then that this old-fashioned Chinese term, which during my childhood used to describe a person who is truthful and good, now signifies someone who is simple-minded, naive and easily taken in. (This new definition is actually in *The Concise Chinese–English Dictionary* published by the Oxford University Press. It is a sad commentary on our times that honesty is now viewed as stupidity.) Nor did I realise that my sister's every gesture of affection towards me was a calculated act of duplicity. By pleading with Niang to be reconciled with Lydia I had in fact 'opened the door to salute the thief' (*kai men yi dao* 開門揖盜). After their rapprochement, it took my sister only two years to poison my stepmother's mind against me.

In the last true conversation I had with my brother James, two days after I discovered that my stepmother had disinherited me, he analysed my predicament very clearly. 'Your problem, Wu Mei [Fifth Younger Sister],' he said, 'is that you're always transferring your own feelings and reasons into others. You wanted to believe that we all shared your dream of a united family. In fact, no one cared except for you.' Then he added, 'When Da Jie [Big Sister] first asked you to help her become reconciled to Niang, did you ever ask yourself about Da Jie's real motivation? Knowing what type of person our sister is, did you really believe that she had undergone a sudden miraculous transformation and was longing to become Niang's caretaker out of the goodness of her heart? Have you never heard of the phrase, "The last one by the sick-bed gets the money"?

'When Da Jie visited you in California, *you* were the one who informed her that Niang was isolated and scared because Father had become senile. On learning this, Da Jie knew immediately that Father's illness would take its toll on Niang. By gaining access to Niang during her weakened state, Da Jie sensed that she could exert enormous influence. And she did.

'I'm only thankful that Da Jie was unsuccessful in her attempts to fly to Hong Kong and nurse Niang in her last illness. If she had done so, I have not the slightest doubt that our Big Sister would have ended up with the entire estate. *Kou mi fu jian* 口蜜腹劍 (Honey on the tongue but dagger in the heart). Da Jie is capable of saying and doing anything for money. Beware of her! She is highly dangerous. In fact, I'm personally convinced that she is in many ways even more evil than Niang.'

To me, more important than keeping in mind that the caretaker in our last illness may exert undue and excessive influence is asking ourselves, 'Will my legacy be boon or bane to my heirs?'

I remember only too well my San Ge 三哥 (Third Elder Brother) James when he first graduated from Cambridge University in the 1960s. Handsome, capable, intelligent and idealistic, he could have succeeded in any given field. Instead, he chose to remain in Hong Kong and work for our parents. Twenty-five years later he was a different man. By then he had invested too much of himself in Father's business and it was too late to leave and strike out on his own. He had run out of ambition and time. Worse, he had become so accustomed to condoning our

224

stepmother's deviousness that he was even willing to compromise his integrity in order to ensure his inheritance.

The most precious gift we can leave our children is not money, but knowledge.

When I was thirteen years old, I had the privilege of spending a few days in the company of my seventy-four-year-old grandfather Ye Ye, who was in poor health and had only seven months to live. On the last morning before I was sent back to my boarding school, Ye Ye gave me this piece of advice: 'You have your whole life ahead of you,' he told me. 'Be smart. Study hard and be independent. I'm afraid the chances of your getting a dowry are slim. Don't end up married off at the age of seventeen like Lydia. You must rely on yourself. No matter what else people may steal from you, they will never be able to take away your knowledge. The world is changing. You must make your own life outside this home.'

It was the last time he spoke to me but I never forgot his words. They gave me hope. Together with his belief in me, that sense of hope lingered throughout my life. It was with me as I sat hunched over my medical textbooks on Saturday nights; crawled out of bed to rush to the hospital in the dead of night; pored over anaesthesia journals on weekends off. It persisted even though my Ye Ye was no longer around, propelling me forever forwards. It became an anchor in my life – a safe and secure harbour that would nourish me for ever.

Besides knowledge, it is essential to provide our children with a sense of integrity, morality and self-worth. By giving them the best education that we can afford, along with the opportunity and motivation to pursue their own future, we will have bestowed upon them an heirloom that is much more significant and valuable than any sum of money. Not only can this bequest never be taken away from them; it is a legacy that will mould their character and influence their behaviour for the rest of their lives.

12

The Lessons of Silence

不言之教

BU YAN ZHI JIAO

My grandfather used to hang two scrolls on the wall above his bed. On each were four Chinese characters he had written with brush and ink. To the left were *Tian jing di yi* 天經地義 and to the right were *Bu yan zhi jiao* 不言之教. Ye Ye was a skilled calligrapher and I could detect the motion of his hand in the shape of the words. Each stroke was like a recording of his thought made manifest through its direction, power or velocity; all the words scripted in a voice uniquely his own.

Once, he saw me sitting on the floor gazing up at the scrolls, transfixed by the deluge of emotion he had managed to transfer on to two sheets of paper.

'Do you know what the words mean, Wu Mei?' he asked.

'Sort of: *tian* 天 means "heaven"; *jing* 經 means "scripture or classic"; *di* 地 means "earth" and *yi* 義 means "justice" or "harmony".'

'Remember them and ponder over them,' he told me. 'Wherever you go in future, think of them from time to time. When you marvel at the beauty of a sunset or become intrigued by the wonders of science, keep in mind that all phenomena on earth are based on *Tian jing di yi* 天經地義 (Heaven's scripture and earth's justice). If inanimate objects without consciousness can contain so much perfection, is it really possible for humans who are endowed with reason to lack an appropriate order?'

'What about the other four words, Ye Ye?'

'Ah! *Bu yan zhi jiao* 不言之教(the lessons of silence)! Those four words were written by Lao Zi in the *Tao Te Ching*. I have been cogitating over them lately. Perhaps, one day, you too will come to appreciate their importance. But that is a discovery you will have to make for yourself . . . when you are ready.'

Fifty years later, I recalled that conversation with my grandfather as I sat in front of the computer to begin the last chapter of *Watching the Tree*. Writing has obliged me to spend long hours searching for those voices which we never hear except when our inner self is at peace and everything else is suspended. I hope that these conclusions, though simple and rudimentary, may bring solace to some who have also been emotionally bludgeoned and are in need of spiritual harmony.

Modern music has been described as a cacophony of din. Children growing up today often do their homework with the television switched on and the radio at full blast. They tell us they can write essays, solve equations and learn chemistry while simultaneously listening to the latest hits, watching game shows and eating dinner. Be that as it may, it seems to me as if our youngsters are fearful of stillness, and are attempting to avoid certain emotions that only descend with the sound of silence.

I remember getting away on an overcast winter afternoon to see a particular Japanese garden in Kyoto: a bare plot of land covered by raked, loose gravel on which stood a few oddly shaped rocks. As I gazed at that spare, minimal arrangement, there came upon me a certain indescribable repose. Yet the sensation was familiar, for I had felt it before.

Living in the teeming cities of Shanghai, Hong Kong, London, New York or Los Angeles, we have become only too accustomed to the constant clamour from across the hall or down narrow alleyways. But sometimes, in the hush late at night or with the dew of early dawn, there suddenly unfolds a special element of serenity. And it is often at these moments that we ask ourselves whether we are hearing in the silence the whisperings of our innermost being. Are these then the tidings proclaimed by China's ancient sages? 'Be still, and know that Heaven is close at hand.'

Musicians, painters and writers spend months and years searching for that elusive and fleeting quality: inspiration. In China we call it *yuan qi* 元氣 (see page 99). What is it? Why is it so sought after? Where does it come from?

I read somewhere that great art lies paradoxically in what the painter chooses to leave out as much as in what he elects to put in. As I get older, I too have come to appreciate more and more the subtle nuances conveyed by our best artists precisely because of that which has been left unstated, unexpressed and unsketched. Think back to the thousands of paintings you've seen, the pieces of music you've listened to, the books you've read, or the hundreds of gardens you've visited. What has stayed in your mind and continues to haunt you?

As I step into the last third of my life, I have come to believe more and more in the power and drama of phrases that have remained unspoken, spaces in pictures left blank, or chords *not* played in a piece of music. Sometimes, I am inclined to wonder whether the function of artists is not to create a scaffolding for that which has deliberately been left void and preserved as empty space.

Ponder on some of civilisation's greatest achievements: whether in music, prose, painting, sculpture or landscape architecture. Remember the torrent of emotions unleashed by King Lear in his repetition of the single word 'Never, never, never, never, never!' after the death of his beloved daughter Cordelia. What about that awesome pause following the first four notes of Beethoven's fifth symphony? Or the magnificent calligraphy wrought by the brush of eminent Tang dynasty scholars? Compare man's most elaborately designed gardens (such as Shanghai's Yu Yuan or Beijing's Summer Palace) to the transcendent simplicity of a waterfall at Lu Shan or the breath-taking splendour of Tibet's soaring mountains. Are we merely attempting to approach the perfection of Nature in the creation of our art? These works that we call inspired, some of which move us to the innermost chambers of our heart – are they speaking to us in the only religious language we seem willing to accept these days? And is this the voice of God?

It is difficult to attain spirituality by clambering up the cold steps of science; just as it is perplexing to explain the *tao* by mere words. Perhaps that is why we should seize those moments when our hearts are touched by something beyond logic, something profound with a suggestion of the divine; something mesmerising that induces in us a condition of reverence and awe.

Indeed, we have all been there before. This longing for

the peace that surpasses all understanding. This search for the everlasting light that is the source of everything good, truthful, beautiful, orderly and intelligent. This special place aspired to by our greatest writers, painters, musicians and philosophers.

So in love are we with *re nau* 熱鬧 (clamour and noise) that we have come to mistake the hubbub of partying for happiness. At times, we may do well to remind ourselves that the two are not synonymous. I have heard celebrities confess to feeling lonely and isolated while surrounded by great crowds. Buried within us are yearnings for intimacy and tranquillity that are easily drowned by stridency.

Unfortunately, in the twenty-first century, the era of acquisition and information, money reigns supreme and Mammon is king. Many have no ideals and no goals except the accumulation of cash. In order to carve out their own piece of the pie, some are willing to abandon their beliefs and their integrity. Yet, in this headlong rush toward possession, we feel an emptiness and a sense of dread. Successful businessmen worth tens of millions of dollars have said to me, 'Now I have made another killing on the market and am worth 50 million instead of 30 million dollars. So what? I was already unable to spend the 30 million. What do I do with the extra 20 million? I have this awful sense of *déjà vu* and boredom. I desire something else other than money, but I don't know what. Surely, there has to be *something* more meaningful and permanent. Can everything truly have happened by chance alone? Is there nothing after death at all? How *dismal* it would be!'

Human beings are unique because of all the animals we alone are conscious that we are alive. In addition, only humans are able to communicate by written and oral language, or possess the foresight to plan for the future. We can also intentionally interact with our environment and alter our surroundings. Our words and actions often transcend our lifespan, producing effects long after we are dead and gone.

In the language of Europe, the original meaning of the words 'soul' and 'spirit' is, in fact, equivalent to the Chinese word *qi*. Both 'soul' and '*qi*' may be considered 'the breath of life'; the principle force or energy that pervades all living creatures.

Because this precious gift of life has been given to us, we have the choice of either blithely accepting the bounty and living from day to day, or asking questions about its meaning. Since consciousness entails responsibility, should we hold ourselves accountable for this favour? And is this accountability the beginning of our quest for philosophical integrity?

When my daughter was five years old, I once cut an apple into ever smaller pieces for her. After a while she asked, 'If you go on cutting and cutting, will the bits of apple get so small that they will all go away and become nothing?'

It has been said that the act of discovery lies not in seeking new views but in finding new eyes. Surprisingly, my five-year-old's logic was not far from the truth. Today, physicists are postulating that everything existing in the universe actually comes from the vibrations of minuscule loops of energy known as 'strings'. This 'super-string' theory is able not only to bridge the gap that has existed for most of the twentieth century between general relativity and quantum mechanics; but also to provide the unified field theory that eluded Einstein for the last thirty years of his life. In addition, it is changing our perceptions.

In the twenty-first century the various religions are gradually coalescing into a single entity. This is known as 'syncretism' or the 'fusion of creeds'. Just as there are no sects in mathematics, leaders as diverse as the Catholic Pope John Paul and the Tibetan Buddhist Dalai Lama are beginning to agree on certain fundamental principles. Pope John Paul proposed that even non-Christian religions are reflections of one truth, because they also represent the universal human aspiration to find an ultimate meaning in God. The Dalai Lama, meanwhile, stated unequivocally in his book *Ethics for the Next Millennium* that he is a 'firm believer in religious pluralism'.

Somewhere it is written that every Chinese wears a Confucian thinking-cap, Taoist robe and Buddhist sandals. Since the publication of *Falling Leaves* I have been inundated with questions about my personal beliefs. One Australian reader wrote, 'I consider authors such as you to be our modern-day prophets.'

I confess that I feel the enormity of my own inadequacy in dealing with such expectations. For so many years I have put spiritual issues aside, in the hope of a miraculous and sudden enlightenment from I know not whom. Goals and horizons undergo significant transformation as we progress along the journey of life.

At my fortieth medical school class reunion, competitive comparisons as to who possessed the bigger house, the better-looking spouse, the brighter offspring or the more distinguished career were no longer made with the same urgency or envy as they had been ten years earlier. Instead, we were more interested in each other's state of health, degree of contentment and tranquillity of soul. Someone speculated that at our fiftieth reunion, surviving members would probably be thrilled just to note that some classmates were still around, regardless of how we felt towards each other in our youth.

Compared with the long period of existence of the animal kingdom, which has been around for hundreds of millions of years, the course of written human history (as excavated by archaeologists) has been woefully brief – a mere five or six or seven thousand years. Yet for much of that time, even before Confucius, men have had this overwhelming urge to search for transcendental truths. Why are we here? How did we arrive? Where are we going?

We are all looking for that mysterious 'something' that we are unable to express. Something greater than the combination of space and time and matter that make up the sum total of our observable universe. Something sublime buried deep within each of us that is interfused with our awareness of *beauty*, *truth*, *goodness* and the *order of Nature*.

Consider *beauty*. What happens to us when we are overwhelmed by the beauty of a work of art, be it a painting, a poem or a piece of music? When we abandon ourselves to such an experience, are we being brought closer to that inexpressible 'something' that we call God? Why do we consider certain works beautiful when we come across them? What exactly *is* great art and how do we recognise it? Against what yardstick are we measuring the quality of an artistic creation?

What about the concept of *truth*? Indeed, we have all been there before. We are given a mathematical equation that we are unable to solve. Finally, after hours of deliberation, our teacher provides us with the answer. As soon as we see it, we know that he is correct. We are amazed and full of admiration for his logic, derived from intelligent reasoning. What *is* reason? What *is* truth? How is it recognised?

Then there is *goodness*. We are all moved by unselfish acts performed out of genuine concern for the welfare of others. Such acts are termed 'spiritual acts' by the Dalai Lama. The word 'conscience' is translated as *liang xin* 良心 (good heart) in Chinese, and *liang xin* has the same validity as the physical laws of nature. It is universal and applies to everyone and to all situations. Right and wrong or good and bad are matters of reason, not expressions of sentiment. When we act out of concern for others and not out of self-interest, we are acting out of our own free will.

In September 1990 I went through a period of deep depression after the death of my stepmother. Ten years earlier I had opposed her wishes in helping the children of my eldest sister Lydia out of China. Behind my back, Lydia and her children secretly poisoned Niang's mind against me and caused her to disinherit me.

I remember the horrible, endless flight from Hong Kong to Los Angeles after attending Niang's funeral and the reading of her will. Hollow-eyed from insomnia and speechless with dismay, I stared blankly at nothing for hour after hour, kicking myself over and over for my naiveté and stupidity in allowing

235

myself to be duped and betrayed. 'How is it possible,' I asked myself, 'that an act of altruistic kindness towards my sister and her children could have produced such disastrous consequences for me? Where is the justice?'

There is a well-known proverb in Chinese that says '*Shan you shan bau*' or 'Goodness will be rewarded with goodness'. The strange thing about justice is that even though man may attempt to obstruct and distort its course, it has a knack of finding its own way. Moral or amoral acts have a tendency to transcend the intentions of their perpetrators and exert effects entirely unforeseen by them.

Against the advice of well-meaning friends and attorneys, I refused to consider legal action. Instead, I channelled my *qi* into doing something positive by writing *Falling Leaves*. The publication of my book has not only given me a new career at this late stage in my life; more importantly, it has provided me with an inner happiness characterised by serenity and contentment. Even though I am in the last third of my life, this is the happiest third by far.

Lastly, let us reflect on *order*. The fact that 'nature is orderly' is self-evident and ubiquitous. Through the study of the genome, we now understand that life is much the same across all the countless millions of existing species. A bacterium shares man's distant origins and a chimpanzee becomes our close cousin. The clusters of genes, known as homeoboxes, that control the development of a fertilised human egg into a baby are similar to those controlling the same process in the chicken's egg that we eat for breakfast. There is an intimate connection between the laws of physics governing our cosmos and those of biology controlling the human organism. Should the physical constant regulating the forces between protons be only slightly different, then all the protons would have turned into helium at the early stages after the Big Bang and there would have been no stars and no life. Einstein himself was convinced that there is order behind all science and all mathematics. Where there is order, there is rationality. Where there is rationality, there is purpose. Where there is purpose, there is hope.

Although it is true that our perception of beauty, truth, goodness and order comes from our senses, the human mind also possesses certain innate conditions against which we process our perceptions. This processing procedure is called *reason*. What we comprehend with our reason is more intelligent (and therefore more real) than what we grasp with our senses. In his daily existence, man strives constantly towards a perfect entity that exists somewhere in his mind whenever he looks for inspiration (*yuan qi*), truth, goodness or order. This 'perfect entity' is an idea innate in each and everyone of us. What *is* this 'perfect entity'? Where does it come from? Is it equivalent to the Buddha-nature mentioned in the Buddhist scriptures; or the *tao* of Lao Zi and Zhuang Zi?

In Zen Buddhism, *nirvana* is another name for the original substance of the Buddha-mind, which is also known as Buddha-nature. Buddhists believe that Buddha-nature is present in everyone. By achieving enlightenment, any person can become a buddha.

By the *tao*, Zhuang Zi meant the 'order of Nature'. He saw the universe (*yu zhou*) from a perspective of eternal time and infinite space and concluded that human life was insignificant in a cosmic context. Everything, he said, obeys its own nature. Eagles soar high into the sky while doves hop from branch to branch. Life and death follow each other in a cycle as inevitable as day and night. All things are one because the *tao* combines them into a single unity.

The Dutch philosopher Spinoza (1632–77) demonstrated in his book *Ethics Geometrically Demonstrated* that all forms of life are subject to the universal laws of Nature. In fact, Spinoza identified God with Nature and reduced everything into a single entity, which he called Substance or God or Nature. The universe is controlled through the laws of Nature. This Nature manifests itself in many forms – physical as well as spiritual forms such as thought and extension. These manifestations are all expressions of God. Hence God is the same as the world and the world is the same as God.

When I first entered medical school in London and began the study of physiology, biochemistry and biophysics, I remember being bowled over by the elegance, beauty and order underlying the inner workings of the human body. At medical school my tutor Dr Karl Decker and I used to hold heated discussions deep into the night while making coffee over the Bunsen burner in his lab. He was an intensely cynical sceptic who was inclined towards atheism. Though I longed to agree with him, I simply could not believe that the surprising facts we were discovering day after day in the course of our meticulously thought-out experiments could have come about by accident and were not planned by a higher intelligence.

Like many others, I have no answer to the questions of why we exist or whether our souls will be reincarnated after death. As Buddhists say, 'Tomorrow or the next life – who can be sure which will come first?' I can't explain why pain and suffering are all around us. In *Falling Leaves* and *Chinese Cinderella*, I tried to paint a truthful portrait of my life and family relationships. In *Watching the Tree* I'm attempting to relate what I have learned from my past. Over the years, however, I have arrived at certain conclusions through my personal reflections that I hope you will find helpful.

I venture to suggest that our minds contain certain innate ideas that contribute to our understanding of the universe perceived through our senses. These ideas are equivalent to the Buddha-nature, the *tao* or Spinoza's Substance. The French mathematician/philosopher Descartes postulated that education is merely the unveiling of a previously imprinted code of laws that already exists within us at birth. The French poet de Musset describes man as 'a fallen angel who remembers the heavens'.* Each human mind may be regarded as a 'spiritual entity', reflecting within itself the experience of the entire universe. Unlike animals, we are intelligent creatures with innate standards of beauty, truth and ethics towards which we strive. There is a planned orderliness and dormant intelligence that we can observe in everything in Nature. Kant wrote, 'Two things fill my mind with ever-increasing awe and wonder: the starry heavens above and the moral law within me.' Over two thousand years earlier Confucius had already spoken these words: 'The moral law exists within and the law of the universe exists without.'

'As you mature as a medical student and delve ever deeper into the world of science,' Dr Decker once told me, 'I predict that

---

* '*L'homme est un ange déchu qui se souvient des cieux.*'

you will be driven to conclude that religion is childish nonsense.'

But this has not happened. On the contrary, my quest for knowledge has convinced me that our world was tailor-made for this most magnificent of gifts that has been bestowed upon us: the gift of life. Nowadays we know that the *tao* of the universe follows rules that are fundamentally computational. Ever since the invention of the symbol zero and the universal acceptance of the Hindu-Arabic numerals as the language of mathematics, we humans have been able to create great, new, abstract concepts out of our imagination – concepts that whisper to us of immortality and a divine intelligence.

Since these concepts came from man's minds, it appears as if human consciousness is on the same wavelength as the *tao* of *tian di* 天地 (Heaven and earth). Galileo wrote in *Il Saggiatore* that the 'great book of the universe' is written in the language of mathematics and can only be understood if we gain knowledge of that language. It continues to astonish me that two magical little symbols, 0 and 1, so simple and yet so elegant, should be able not only to represent an infinite diversity of numbers, but also to describe the entire cosmos.

After China reopened her doors in 1979, my husband and I made a special trip to Shandong province and climbed the 6293 granite steps leading to the summit of the sacred mountain of Taishan. On our way up, I came across two rows of Chinese characters carved out of the surface of a rock. The four words of the first row, *Bu yan zhi jiao* 不言之教, were familiar. I had seen them many times before on the scroll above my Ye Ye's bed. The five words on the second row, *Tian xia xi ji zhi* 天下希及之, were new to me. I read the two phrases out loud to myself, and their meaning reached me like a revelation of the quietness all around: 'The lessons of silence are peerless and are unmatched by anything else under Heaven.' I recalled that in ancient China, Taishan mountain was considered to be holy ground, and was worshipped like a symbol of Heaven. As I gazed down at the rocky ridges and peaks rising and falling like the spines of huge dragons stretched out along the vast peninsula below, there came upon me an absolute certainty that the great stillness surrounding me had a divine significance. Suddenly, in the majestic hush of the early morning air, I understood what my Ye Ye was trying to say so many years ago. At that moment, I felt the overwhelming presence of God and knew that He was there: *in the silence.*

AUTHOR'S NOTE

I have read widely during the writing of this book, in addition to my own studies I found the following books of great interest and would recommend them to anyone who wants to read further on the subject.

Lao Tze *Tao Te Ching*
Baynes, W. (translator) *I Ching*
Arthur Waley (translator) *Tao Te Ching*
Sun Zi *The Art of War*
Zhuang Zi

Lun Yu *Confucian Analects*
Lin Yu-tang *My Country and My People*
Lin Yu-Tang *The Importance of Living*
Chan Wing Tait *A Source Book on Chinese Philosophy*

Joseph Needham *Science and Civilization in China*
Mattei Ricci *China in the Sixteenth Century*
Arnold H. Rowbotham *Missionary and Mandarin*
Robert Temmple *The Genius of China*
Anthony Thwaite *The Selected Letters of Philip Larkin (1940–1985)*
Arthur Waley *Three Ways of Thought in Ancient China*

Some of the translations from the original Chinese were based on the above books.

INDEX

246

phytochemicals 127
*Platform Scriptures of the Sixth
    Patriarch, see Liu Zu Tan
    Jing*
Polo, Marco 162
polyphenols 130
polytheism 74
power, political 179–80
Pritikin diet 121–2
privacy 178–9, 180
psychology, and language 176
psychotherapy, Jungian 25–6
Pure Land Buddhists 86

qi 11, 20, 41, 86, 97–110, 232
    and *feng shui* 184, 189,
        200–201
    and food 122
    and medicine 124
qi gong 22, 41, 86, 156
Qian Long, Emperor 61, 179
Qin Shi Huang Di, Emperor 4, 37
Qing dynasty 4, 59, 61, 162, 179
Qu Yuan 112
quantum mechanics 23, 106, 108,
    232

reality 175
reason 237
Red Guards 5, 24
red yeast 132
reincarnation 10, 54, 75, 77
Reine, Aunt 135
relativity 23, 33, 36, 75, 105, 175,
    232–3
    Einstein's theory of 36, 40, 105,
        108
religion 9, 233–4, 237–41
Ricci, Matteo 56, 61, 62, 162, 193
Rites controversy 53

Saggiatore, Il (Galileo) 240
Schall von Bell, Adam 193–4
scholar-philosophers 56, 62–4
School of Sudden Enlightenment
    87–8

science 9, 62, 68, 157–8, 160–2,
    236–7
    see also physics
Science and Civilization in China
    (Needham) 198
Second Great Buddhist Council 78
Selected Letters of Philip Larkin (ed.
    Thwaite) 31
self-awareness 85, 89–90, 94
self-examination 25–6, 27
Seng Chao (Buddhist monk) 80, 82,
    85
sexual practices 41
Shang dynasty 166
Shanghai 3–4, 6
Shao Yung 24–5
Shen Gua 142, 196
Shen Xiu 88
Shi Ji (Si Ma Qian) 57, 126
Si Ma Qian 57
silence 228–9, 241
Silvester II, Pope 159
Singapore 69, 199
social consciousness 68–9
social relationships 48
social status 48, 49–50, 64–7
sociology, Confucian 47–8
Song dynasty 51, 57, 65, 142,
    196
Sosigenes 206
South-East Asia 69
South Korea 21
sovereign 48, 55, 104
Soviet Union 5
soya 125–8
Spinoza, Benedict de 34, 238
spirits 47, 53
Sri Lanka 77, 78
Stein, Sir Arthur 89
subatomic physics 23, 36
Sun Se-miao 120
Sun Yat-sen 4
Sun Zi 103–5, 109
super-string theory 23, 108, 232
superstition 40–41, 202, 203
syncretism 233

守 株 待 兔